D1599214

Dionne Brand

The Blue Clerk

Ars Poetica in 59 Versos

DUKE UNIVERSITY PRESS

DURHAM AND LONDON

Printed in the United States on acid-free paper ∞

Aphid illustration by duncan1890, Getty Images
Designed by CS Richardson
Typeset in Huronia by M&S, Toronto
Cover art: © subjug. E+, Getty Images.

Library of Congress Cataloging-in-Publication Data
Names: Brand, Dionne, [date] author.
Title: The blue clerk : ars poetica in 59 versos / Dionne Brand.
Description: Durham : Duke University Press, 2018.
Includes bibliographical references and index.
Identifiers: LCCN 2018019511 (print)
LCCN 2018027042 (ebook)
ISBN 9781478002055 (ebook)
ISBN 9781478000068 (hardcover : alk. paper)
Classification: LCC PR9199.3. B683 (ebook)
LCC PR9199.3.B683 B5 2018 (print)
DDC 811/.54—DC23
LC record available at https://lccn.loc.gov/2018019511

THE BLUE CLERK

ONE

STIPULE
A small leaf-like appendage to a leaf

I have left this unsaid. I have withheld. What is withheld
is the left-hand page. Nine left-hand pages have already
written their own left-hand pages, as you will see. They
are chronic. I have withheld more than I have written.
Evergreen and deciduous. Incurable. And uneasy, and like
freight.

VERSO 1
The back of a leaf

What is withheld is on the back. A stack, a ream.

There are bales of paper on a wharf somewhere; at a port, somewhere. There is a clerk inspecting and abating them. She is the blue clerk. She is dressed in a blue ink coat, her right hand is dry, her left hand is dripping; she is expecting a ship. She is preparing. Though she is afraid that by the time the ship arrives the stowage will have overtaken the wharf.

The sea off the port is roiling some days, calm some days.

Up and down the wharf the clerk examines the bales, shifts old left-hand pages, making room for the swift, voluminous, incoming freight.

The clerk looks out sometimes over the roiling sea or over the calm sea, finding the horizon, seeking the transfiguration of a ship.

The bales have been piling up for years yet they look brightly scored, crisp and cunning. They have abilities the clerk is forever curtailing and marshalling. They are stacked deep and high and the clerk, in her inky garment, weaves in and out of them checking and rechecking that they do not find their way onto the right-hand page. She scrutinizes the manifest hourly, the contents and sequence of loading. She keeps account of cubic metres of senses, perceptions, and resistant facts. No one need be aware of these; no one is likely to understand. Some of these are quite dangerous.

And, some of them are too delicate and beautiful for the present world.

There are green unclassified aphids, for example, living with these papers.

The sky over the wharf is a sometime-ish sky, it changes with the moods and anxieties of the clerk, it is ink blue as her coat or grey as sea or pink as evening clouds. It is cobalt as good luck or manganite as trouble.

The sun is a red wasp that flies in and out of the clerk's ear. It escapes the clerk's flapping arms.

The clerk would like a cool moon but all the weather depends on the left-hand pages. All the acridity in the salt air, all the waft of almonds and seaweed, all the sharp, poisonous odour of time.

The left-hand pages swell like dunes in some years. It is all the clerk can do to mount them with her theodolite, to survey their divergent lines of intention. These dunes would envelop her as well as the world if she were not the ink-drenched clerk.

Some years the aridity of the left-hand pages makes the air pulver, parches the hand of the clerk. The dock is then a desert, the bales turned to sand, and then the clerk must arrange each grain in the correct order, humidify them with her breath, and wait for the season to pass.

And some years the pages absorb all the water in the air, tumid like four-hundred-year-old wet wood, and the dock weeps and creaks and the clerk's garment sweeps sodden through the bales and the clerk weeps and wonders why she is here and when will a ship ever arrive.

I am the clerk, overwhelmed by the left-hand pages.
Each blooming quire contains a thought selected out of
many reams of thoughts and stripped by me, then presented
to the author. (The clerk replaces the file, which has grown
with touch to a size unimaginable.)

I am the author in charge of the ink-stained clerk pacing
the dock. I record the right-hand page. I do nothing really
because what I do is clean. I forget the bales of paper
fastened to the dock and the weather doesn't bother me.
I choose the presentable things, the beautiful things.
And I enjoy them sometimes, if not for the clerk.

The clerk has the worry and the damp thoughts and the
arid thoughts.

Now where will I put that new folio, she says. There's no
room where it came from, it's withheld so much about . . .
never mind; that will only make it worse.

The clerk goes balancing the newly withheld pages
across the ink-slippery dock. She throws an eye on the still
sea; the weather is concrete today; her garment is stiff like
marl today.

STIPULE

I saw the author, her left cheek, her left shoulder agape,
a photo of her washed in emergency, a quieting freight, a
grandfather, a great-grandmother, one stage of an illness, on
the rim of a page without verbs, bullet-ridden and elegant,
a boulder beside her, the things collected in her brain, green
lacewing larvae, mourning cloak, bryozoa, aphids (aphids),
ladybird, *Echinopsis* and wisteria and rooms, the manifest
green, unclassified ways of saying let us go, the small blue
book of the author's thoughts to decipher, gradatios of
violet, blue and black, the clerk, I, need lemon, a spanner,
a vehicle, a bowl of nails, a wire, a cup, a lamp, the clerk
knows where the salt, where the sugar, where the flowers,
the museums and corpses, same number with the
following, are we not human unnumbered, poignard case,
a horse, a plummet

When Borges says he remembers his father's library in
Buenos Aires, the gaslight, the shelves, and the voice of his
father reciting Keats's "Ode to a Nightingale," I recall the
library at the roundabout on Harris Promenade. The library
near the Metro Cinema and the Woolworths store. But to
go back, when my eyes lit first on Borges's dissertation I
thought, I had no Library. And I thought this thought with
my usual melancholy and next my usual pride in living
without.

And the first image that came to me after that was my
grandfather's face with his tortoiseshell spectacles and his
weeping left eye and his white shirt and his dark seamed
trousers and his newspaper and his moustache and his
clips around his shirt sleeves and his notebooks and his
logbooks; and at the same moment that the melancholy
came it was quickly brushed aside by the thought that he
was my library.

In his notebooks, my grandfather logged hundredweight
of copra, pounds of chick feed and manure; the health of
horses, the nails for their iron shoes; the acreages of coconut
and tania; the nuisance of heliconia; the depth of two rivers;
the length of a rainy season.

Then I returned to Harris Promenade and the white
library with wide steps, but when I ask, there was no white
library with wide steps, they tell me, but an ochre library at
a corner with great steps leading up. What made me think
it was a white library? The St. Paul's Anglican Church

anchoring the lime white Promenade, the colonial white
Courthouse, the grey white public hospital overlooking
the sea? I borrowed a book at that white library even
though the library as I imagine it now did not exist. A book
by Gerald Durrell, namely, *My Family and Other Animals.*
I don't remember any other books I brought home, though
I remember a feeling of quiet luxury and a desire for
spectacles to seem as intelligent as my grandfather.

And I read here, too, in this white library a scrap about
Don Quixote and Sancho Panza, though only the kind
of scrap, the kind of refuse, or onion skin, they give
schoolchildren in colonial countries about a strange
skinny man on a horse with a round sidekick. The clerk
would say I could use this, but I can't.

The ochre library on Harris Promenade was at the spot
that was called "Library Corner" and it used to be very
difficult to get to because of the traffic and the narrow
sidewalk. But I was agile and small. And I thought I was
ascending a wide white-stepped library. And though that
was long ago, I remember the square clock tower adjacent
to the roundabout. And I can see the Indian cinema next
door, papered with the film *Aarti* starring Meena Kumari
and Ashok Kumar.

My grandfather with his logs and notebooks lived in a
town by the sea. That sea was like a lucent page to the left
of the office where my grandfather kept his logs and his
notebooks with their accounts. Apart from the depth of the
two rivers, namely the Iguana and the Pilot, he also noted
the tides and the times of their rising and falling.

moonrise	*5.34 a.m.*	
high tide	*5.48 a.m.*	*0.82 ft*
sunrise	*5.56 a.m.*	
low tide	*12.40 p.m.*	*0.03 ft*
new moon	*4.45 p.m.*	
sunset	*6.23 p.m.*	
high tide	*6.33 p.m.*	*0.56 ft*
low tide	*12.02 a.m.*	*0.16 ft*

Spring tides, the greatest change between high and low. Neap tides, the least.

And, the rain, he recorded, the number of inches and its absence. He needed to know about the rain for sunning and drying the copra. And, too, he kept a log of the sun, where it would be and at what hour, and its angle to the earth in what season. And come to think of it he must have logged the clouds moving in. He said that the rain always came in from the sea. The clouds moving in were a constant worry. I remember the rain sweeping in, pelting down like stones. That is how it used to be said, the rain is pelting down like stones. He filled many logbooks with rain and its types: showers, sprinkles, deluges, slanted, boulders, pebbles, sheets, needles, slivers, pepper. Cumulonimbus clouds. Or, Nimbostratus clouds. Convection rain and relief rain. *Relief rain* he wrote in his logbook in his small office, and the rain came in from the sea like pepper, then pebbles, then boulders. It drove into his window and disturbed his logs with its winds and it wet his desk. And he or someone else would say, "But look at rain!" And someone else would say, "See what the rain do?" As if the rain were human. Or they would say, "Don't let that rain come in here." As if the rain were a creature.

Anyway, my grandfather had a full and thorough record of clouds and their seasons and their violence.

From under the sea a liquid hand would turn a liquid page each eight seconds. This page would make its way to the shore and make its way back. Sometimes pens would wash up onto the beach, long stem-like organic styli. We called them pens; what tree or plant or reef they came from we did not know. But some days the beach at Guaya would be full of these styli just as some nights the beach would be full of blue crabs. Which reminds me now of García Márquez's old man with wings but didn't then as I did not know García Márquez then and our blue crabs had nothing to do with him. It is only now that the crabs in his story have overwhelmed my memory. It is only now that my blue night crabs have overwhelmed his story. Anyway we would take these pens and sign our names, and the names of those we loved, along the length of the beach. Of course these names rubbed out quickly, and as fast as we could write them the surf consumed them. And later, much much later, I learned those pens were *Rhizophora mangle* propagules.

What does this have to do with Borges? Nothing at all. I walked into the library and it was raining rain and my grandfather's logs were there, and the wooden window was open. As soon as I opened the door, down the white steps came the deluge. If I could not read I would have drowned.

Now you are sounding like me, the clerk says. I am you, the author says.

VERSO 2

I can't say I was conscious of the left-hand page as early as this but there it was if I had looked. There it was, if you had looked, says the clerk. Essentially years and years actually trying to write in the centre of your life, working with all the intelligence of your being. The feeling of repelling some invasion in order, one day, to be yourself. *Rhizophora mangle* propagules fell into the mangrove lagoon near the Iguana River, where the sea carried them to us.

The sea brought, too, blue-red kilometres of *Physalia physalis.*

Then I had six shields in the ground, I thought I'd grow a
little corn or take care of a rabbit—both for food. Then I
saw a column of orange air, is what I saw. Then I saw a
river. I remembered the river. I remember the garbage. I saw
a column of night. I remember a whale. What is a pillow
tree? I saw pebbles in the dry riverbed. I saw yellow. What
kind of yellow? Mars yellow. Iron yellow. I saw polished
pebbles. I heard *quarrel, quarrel, quarrel* underfoot, when
you walked. Then I ran back to the road. I didn't think
much of the meaning of life, I only thought of my way
through it. Then I saw a green window held open with
a stick. What green? Oxide of chromium, terre verte,
malachite.

There's a woman leaving by boat to go to the house where
she would have an abortion, and then a story of a woman
returning by plane to the hobble of family, and then
another about a woman who was taken up by the goddess
of winds, storms, and waterfalls, and another about a
woman who knelt in the middle of a city street praying,
and another about a woman who sat at a small table with a
lamp looking at the insects it attracted, then fell asleep and
was awakened by a screaming bird. Then there was the
story about a woman on a gritting train to Montreal and a
wraith, a racist screed veering toward her on the escalator
at the Gare Centrale and a woman who sat at a bar in
Kensington Market and saw the ghost of Cristóbal Colón.
(All these women were embattled except perhaps for the
woman in a story who had lovely breasts, adored by many
schoolgirls.)

VERSO 2.2.1

On the train, is that when I should say the clerk emerged?
She was before me, she was always with me. She was a
stevedore stowing cargo for one of my grandmothers, Luisa
Andrade from Venezuela. I met her on Luisa's piano with
the photographs. But that was in another language. Luisa
threw a man into a pit and covered him with sand; when
he got up she had mothered his six children, stitched racial
discord among them, subjected them to photographs for
the piano and left for her grave. She came from La Guaira
on a steamer on the 18th of a certain month. You are
making that up. Well Cumaná then. Guaira. She became
legend. I did not know her name until a few years ago.
You never asked. She was legend.

VERSO 2.3

There was a second woman and she was a woman of the book, a woman of diaries, and a woman of such compact violence that in an instant, brief as it was, she fell in love with the woman of forbidding language. No one has asked me about her.

And then there was one, another woman who did not want
to be in the world, or the world she was dragged into, who
noticed right away the fatal harm but who gave birth to a
woman who wanted to be in the world true and absolutely
whole and therefore lived with ghosts since that world
could not happen yet. And both of them, all they could do
was give birth to fragments of their possible selves and
then more fragments of themselves would sit in a window
on Bethlehemsteeg in Amsterdam or burst with lust in San
Fernando or write long letters of excuses in Toronto, until
the last of them returned to the ghosts of the second. These
two women even when they gave birth to men the men
were women. That is. They were undone by something or
other and lay on apartment floors gurgling up some
exhaustion with masculinity or killed that exhaustion in
some violent Greyhound flight from Miami to New York.
And the men who read them said they wanted something
much more heroic, as if they weren't yet fed up with a
heroism that distorted them, as if they weren't yet gagging
on a heroism that left them right where they were. As if
they were not maimed with heroism, as if their eyes were
not closed and bruised. Or else they wanted themselves
written as Caliban over and over and over again, they loved
him perpetually, the way he stayed helper and prodigal
brother to Prospero, the way his sores remained open, the
way Prospero stabbed him.

VERSO 2.4

All your women, I notice now, leave on boats to get
abortions, or leave by poisoning from their own hands, or
sit gazing at insects, or leave in flights over cliffs, or leave
by their imagination but leave trying to attend to their own
intelligence, "but" for the love of god, they'd be human.

VERSO 2.5

I had a great-grandmother, Angelina, who fled in a pirogue
across the four Bocas del Dragón. From the ragged coast of
one island to the ragged coast of another. She fled with her
lover and her three children. Her husband swore to kill her
and her new man. The waters in the Bocas are perilous.
Between Huevos, Monos, Chacachacare. I can see her
standing in the prow as in a painting, her lover—a shadow
of herself; because it is she taking the risk of murder; he
only loves her and will be the father of several more
children but she will leave him too. A watercolour. The sea
is verdigris, her head scarf is ochre, her dress is lead white,
her three children arrayed around her skirt tail—the two
boys in khaki, the little girl, my grandmother, Amelia, in
red flowers.

I came to the city and it wasn't the city yet. It wasn't any place and I began there. It wasn't any place and I was no one and it began there and I began there. At the edge of the city, at Keele and Bloor, there was nothing but a subway and a police car. And to tell by my poetry there's always a policeman and a hyphen and there are many languages and many signs, which is why there is a policeman to manage the hyphen and to manage the languages and to manage the signs. The city has no contours yet and no buildings, that is why there's a bicycle in some poems, and a syntax bunched like a new wall, and then a syntax drifting out to the northern fractured sea and to the southern enclosed sea. There is a trio of women on a corner waiting for time to start them and a man who falls down a staircase when the policeman shoots him. There's the author, the clerk, the poet, that *flâneur*, collecting streets, and there are uncollectible streets and places and temporary streets and places; the bell of markets and the rake of money making temporary streets and places uncollectible. There's the eager lyric vowing it all has never happened before, hoping it all has never happened before, and straightaway writing the book, the city disappearing in it.

Yesterday, I heard, at the Nosso Talho Butcher Shop, a
transaction—$52.50 for forty pounds of chicken legs—
and it was in two dialects of Spanish and two dialects of
English and someone was listening in Urdu. Or was it
Punjabi? Chali pon kuku dyain lata, bauth maengi hai(n).
And in a series of languages this is good news. Molto
economiche (Italian). Muito baratos (Brazilian Portuguese).
Ponde arte al lado, e baratisimo. Baratisimo, baratisimo.
Putting art aside, that's really cheap, very cheap.

At first there's no lake in the city, at first there are only
elevators, at first there are only constricting office desks;
there are small apartments and hamburger joints and
unpaid telephone bills. Then a few nightclubs appear and
eventually the lake disinters. At times there's a highway
and a car and friends in a snowstorm heading nowhere but
back to the city and Sarah Vaughan is singing in the cabin
of the car. The three of us are frightened of everything.
Our lives in this town, which is not a town, and on this
snow road, which is no road, who will protect us. In the
city there is no simple love or simple fidelity, the poem
long after concludes. There's a slippery heart that abandons.
Fists are full of women's bodies. The Group of Seven is
painting just outside the city now. The graffiti crew is here
inside blowing up the expressway and the city is like a
Romare Bearden or a Basquiat. More Basquiat. The cynical
clerk notes, in her cynical English, all the author has elided,
the diagonal animosities and tiers of citizenship. The
author wants a cosmopolitan city. Nothing wrong with
that. But the clerk who orbits her skull has to deal with all
the animus.

The author's not naive, far from it, but however compli-
cated she is, the clerk is more so. The clerk notices there are
air raids, a lingua of sirens and gunshots in the barracking
suburbs, the incendiary boys are rounded up by incendiary
boys and babies are falling from fifteen-storey buildings
into the shrubbery; each condo fights for the view of the

exhumed lake, until the sky is cloudy with their shadow. The atmosphere is dull with petulant cars. The author avoids all this; you see my point?

The girl on the bicycle says (there is always a girl on a
bicycle because the author cannot ride a bicycle, so one
time the girl on the bicycle she rode all across the city and
the streets were like the ribs of an eel). "Some eel have
saltwater beginnings. Spending their mature lives in lakes.
Some eel are electric." The girl, in the book to come,
wonders why we never collect beauty; as she sits, collecting
beauty at a window on the lake. She answers, "La belleza
no hace daño. / Sac dep khong hai nguoi. / Mei mao boo
hai ren. / Ang kagan / dahan ay nindi nasisira." It doesn't
leave its broken claw in your neck bone.

The author scrapes and scrapes. A palimpsest. The old city resurfaces. Its old self, barely concealed, lifts its figure off the page, heaves deep sighs of bigotry. This beast will never die, the clerk breathes.

The taxi drivers know this. "Miss," one of them says, "don't talk about this city, I know this city. You come here thinking, you'll do this for a year, maybe two, before you know it, it's ten years. And what did I used to do, and what did I hope, I can't tell you. I can't talk about it. It's no use."

In the back of the cab a poet tries to sympathize. "I know, I know."

"You don't know, Miss."

And I don't. I do know that we are both only trying to make a way through life. We are not trying to make sense of it any longer. And I am lucky to be the poet in the cab. I do not know his life. With me this will find its way to a silver-struck enjambment of regret. He will make his way to regret itself.

The woman who lives with him; and the children who live with him? I wonder how this melancholy has scored them.

Nights later another driver tells you, "Miss, no, no, no, women are not equal to men. No, no, you don't understand. You have to understand; every holy book. Miss, Bible or Koran, not possible. It's okay, you're a nice lady, very intelligent but no. You have to learn this, Miss."

He looks back at me with a pity, as if, if I don't learn this my life will be hard and I will be punished. He's telling me for my own good.

That cab ride sends the clerk into a polemical frenzy. She opens my notebook and writes the following rant: *Modernity can spread a bed of weaponry to what it calls the far reaches of the globe but it cannot spread women's equality. It cannot stem the liquidity of capital, it cannot even feed its own populations but female bodies are still trophy to tradition and culture.* The clerk marks this down. I cannot use it. The actual true elevation above sea level, the clerk says. What is that to me, I ask. This is the ranging rod, she says, shod with iron.

The clerk fills a small, thick red moleskin that swallows five hours of time. *The empires,* she fumes, *the empires called culture and religion only have one province left— women.* Her notebook is sleepless.

But no, thinks the optimistic author, not just; another cab ride—we talked about Gabriel García Márquez and another we spoke of Camara Laye, then waiting at a stoplight we assessed the IMF and then, in the same breath, the way the autumn arrived between Thursday and Sunday last week. So? The clerk is quiet with condolences for a moment.

One cab ride can catapult you into melancholy, another can sprout wires from your brain. The author must erase this notebook with snow and snows and snows and trains, and febrile women.

VERSO 3.4

In this city, you fall in love at Chester subway, it's not a beautiful subway so your love makes it so. But its ugliness may doom your love, and you know it but you love anyway.

VERSO 3.5

The subway skeletons its way east, west. North like
anxious electrocardiogram, there are invisible stations. At
least that is what the author says. Like the eel, bone black,
calcined.

VERSO 3.6

In the book to come two new men are trying to arrive in another time, subatomic particles rapid as light along the DVP, a woman is on a train leaving again for Montreal, trying to enter yet another syntax. The clerk expects a sloop of war from across the water. Always.

VERSO 3.7

The city in the book to come is full of people who think there's a trick to everything. And they're right of course, the clerk reproaching, after all, twenty mobile phone companies own the electromagnetic spectrum and can sell you a signed two-year contract for the infrared direction and speed at which light travels; some can sell you lightning itself. The author measures the tectonic plates of condos, leaving one apartment for another, one city block for another. The author and the poet always have to leave somewhere, someone, themselves. Only the energies of cities might cool them, metamorphose them.

VERSO 3.8

The clerk senses an urgency in the author, the author is
always rushing somewhere.

There are five ways of saying let us go home, the clerk tells
the author.

inakeen aan guriga aadnee hadeer (standard, the clerk says)
udgoonoow = sweet-smelling one
aqalkii aan u kacno hadatan (middle dialect, the clerk says)
indhoquruxoow = beautiful eyes
ar soo bax aan xaafadii hadeerbo tagnee (banaadiri)
qalbiwanaagoow = good-hearted one.

On the other hand, "home" as roots or a place where one
feels at home would be:
inakeen aan dhulkii hooyo aadnee hadeer (standard, the
clerk says)
nakeen aan maandeeq soo haybanee hada (northern, the
clerk says).

You understand, says the clerk, which will you use? You
keep them, says the author. The clerk climbs into the
packet boat.

*To verse, to turn, to bend, to plough, a furrow, a row, to turn
around, toward, to traverse*

When I was nine coming home one day from school, I
stood at the top of my street and looked down its gentle
incline, toward my house obscured by a small bend, taking
in the dipping line of the two-bedroom scheme of houses,
called Mon Repos, my rest. But there I've strayed too far
from the immediate intention. When I was nine coming
home from school one day, I stood at the top of my street
and knew, and felt, and sensed looking down the gentle
incline with the small houses and their hibiscus fences,
their rosebush fences, their ixora fences, their yellow and
pink and blue paint washes; the shoemaker on the left
upper street, the dressmaker on the lower left, and way to
the bottom the park and the deep culvert where a boy on a
bike pushed me and one of my aunts took a stick to his
mother's door. Again, when I was nine coming home one
day in my brown overall uniform with the white blouse, I
stood on the top of my street knowing, coming to know in
that instant when the sun was in its four o'clock phase and
looking down I could see open windows and doors and
front door curtains flying out. I was nine and I stood at the
top of the street for no reason except to make the descent
of the gentle incline toward my house where I lived with
everyone and everything in the world, my sisters and my
cousins were with me, we had our bookbags and our four
o'clock hunger with us and our grandmother and every-
thing we loved in the world were waiting in the yellow

washed house, there was a hibiscus hedge and a buttercup bush and zinnias waiting and for several moments all this seemed to drift toward the past; again when I was nine and stood at the head of my street and looked down the gentle incline toward my house in the four o'clock coming-home sunlight, it came over me that I was not going to live here all my life, that I was going away and never returning some day. A small wind brushed everything or perhaps it did not but afterward I added a small wind because of that convention in movies, but something like a wave of air, or a wave of time passed over the small street or my eyes, and my heart could not believe my observation, a small wind passed over my heart drying it and I didn't descend the gentle incline and go home to my house and my grandmother and tell her what had happened, I didn't enter the house that was washed with yellow distemper that we had painted on the previous Christmas, I didn't enter the house and tell her how frightened I was by the thought I had at the top of our street, the thought of never living there, which seemed as if it meant never having existed, or never having known her, I never told her the melancholy I felt or the intrusion the thought represented. I never descended that gentle incline of the street toward my house, the I who I was before that day went another way, she disappeared and became the I who continued on to become who I am. I do not know what became of her, where she went, the former I who separated once we came to the top of the street and looked down and something like a breeze that would be added later after watching many movies passed over us. What became of her, the one who gave in so easily or was she so surprised to find that thought that would overwhelm her so, and what made her keep quiet. When I was nine and coming home one day, my street changed just as I stood at the top of it and I knew I would never live there again or all my life. The thought altered the afternoon and my life and after that I was in a hurry to leave. There was another consciousness waiting for a little girl to grow up and think future thoughts, waiting for some years to pass and some obligatory life to be lived until I would arrive here. When I was nine I left myself and entered myself. It was at the top of the street, the street was called MacGillvary Street, the number was twenty-one, there were zinnias in the front yard and a buttercup bush with milky sticky pistils we used to stick on our faces. After that all the real voices around me became subdued and I was impatient and dissatisfied with everything, I was hurrying to my life and I stood outside of my life. I never arrived at my life, my life became always standing outside of my life and looking down its incline and seeing the houses as if in a daze. It was a breeze, not a wind, a kind of slowing of the air, not a breeze, a suspension of the air when I was nine standing at the top of MacGillvary Street about to say something I don't know what and turning about to run down. No, my grandmother said never to run pell-mell down the street toward the house as ill-behaved people would, so I was about to say something, to collect my cousins and sisters into an orderly file and to walk down to our hibiscus-fenced house with the yellow outer walls and my whole life inside. A small bit of air took me away.

In June, I realized I had already abandoned nation long
before I knew myself, the author says. That attachment
always seemed like a temporary hook in the shoulder
blade. A false feeling, in a false moment. Just like when one
April in the year I turned eight, I noticed I had been put in
a yellow dress. Ochre yellow? asks the clerk. Yellow ochre.
Iridium oxide. But all around me everyone seemed to feel
it, this nation/girl. I thought of the dress as a beheading. I
had moments of loneliness when I could not feel it also.
And I felt as if I were betraying many people all at once.
And everyone said one had to feel it so I felt it like when
reading a book one feels a feeling, but it is in a book and
not in one's real life. But I could not understand the
agreements everyone else had made to the feelings in the
book, the fears of dispossessions. I must have started
dispossessed then, the clerk says.

Every year for forty years I've been asked the same
question by someone who needed to consume allegiances.
Some interrogator observes my skin and asks me why.
Every year I've answered into a void like Coltrane blowing
"Venus" out into the nothing. Like Ornette Coleman
cooking sciences. And sometimes I've tried not making the
interrogator feel bad, or I fend off the attack with dissem-
bling. Most times (every time, the clerk mumbles) I haven't
done what I should, which is to rise and leave like my
women. Sail off on a boat, leap off a cliff, or just sit and sip
my beer at the old Lisbon Plate in Kensington Market.

These tedious questions have drawn this line in my left cheek; they've nailed this pain in my left shoulder. Every time, the clerk says loudly.

I am speaking here of something you would not understand as a clerk. No I wouldn't, nods the clerk. None of it makes sense. Your sense-making apparatus is invisible to me, says the clerk, or at least I would like to keep it invisible. It is like tracing paper over tracing paper. I don't use tracing paper.

VERSO 5.0.1

What the author has. A line in her left cheek, a pain in her left shoulder, a crushed molar, an electric wire running from her elbow to her smallest left finger. Wings in her left eye.

VERSO 5.1

In December, any December, standing in Elmina, the dirt
floor, the damp room of the women's cells, nation loses all
vocabulary. Loses its whole alphabet. I have no debts.
I have no loves. A soccer game every four years; maybe
that. I have two eyes that see where the body that carries
them sleeps. I have the drama of skies, no question; an
affinity for blue that makes me fill beautiful bottles with
blue watercolour and water, that's a habit. Of course the
earth is beneath your feet and so there must be place or the
feeling of place or gravity. But which nation ever said of a
woman she is human? So what allegiances do you have?
Temporary and provisional, wherever.

　　So what? You feel featherless, the clerk says. Didn't
you always; weren't you just an outrider? You tried to fit
in, to your own demise though, you rode shotgun to your
own disaster, she says. You're right. No need for violent
metaphor, the author cautions. Again, let me draw your
attention to the tracing paper.

Soon in August I saw a woman come into the beauty
parlour, she hadn't been sane for years but she came in, in a
lucid moment, lucid for what we call sane. She asked the
woman standing at my hair, "How much is the wig?" The
women gently told her $49.95. Then she said with a wistful
sigh, "I want a ponytail," and the woman showed her a
ponytail, as if she were a real customer. I've turned this into
something else weeks after, but the hairdresser, Base, was
gentle with the woman, the most kind thing I'd seen all
day, pretending the woman was sane. But then it struck me
later that the mad woman's moment of lucidity was the
entranceway to women's madness on the earth. The beauty
parlour—what a narrow doorway, what a pitiful place. On any
other day the mad woman would be nude at Lansdowne
and Bloor with her dress lifted over her head or tied as a belt
around her waist. On any other day. These two things, nude
on the street or the beauty parlour. I was in the beauty
parlour, there myself sane as ever, shaking my head at the
mad woman. I just haven't the courage to be nude on the
street like her. Someone will come up to me after this and
ask, "But isn't there some middle ground, but surely we can
try to exist, but aren't you happy sometimes?" I hate this
"someone." If you like. Whoever you are. But don't be
annoying. I've answered that already. Just because you have
only stage one of an illness doesn't mean you're well. Yes
you could have a fever, yes you could be dead, no doubt that
would be worse. But recognize the disease.

VERSO 5.2.1

What the author has, one stage of an illness, what illness, an earache, steady, an inclination to take her leave of places after an hour or so. A gregariousness followed by a sharp desire to be alone.

VERSO 5.5

I have plans; I have no plans. They disappear in the Gulf of
Mexico like brown pelicans and hermit crabs in an oil spill.
Isn't it time we stopped saying *spill*? That wasn't a spill it
was a deluge. It has no mercy, nation. I have no mercy. I'm
jaundiced. All the while through the hoots of democracy, I
was looking for the women in Tahrir Square, in Yemen, in
Tunisia. I am listening. Whatever, the author says. I don't
want to hear any more about waiting. In September, and
now October, I am unpinned from all allegiances. Of course
you're not. But what if I wrote like this? Unpinned.

Au coin de la rue des Ursulines et François Xavier the author notices a luminous sky. It must have been there always. And what am I doing here. Grey minister, grey petrol, grey detour, the clerk answers. Where life leads you it is not so much impossible to know but to anticipate. No that is a lie, one chooses, one anticipates, one chooses among a certain number of anticipations; one anticipates among a certain set of choices. How it goes. How will I get out.

What the author needs, an epiphonema: "The Taxonomy of Crop Pests: The Aphids" by Miller and Foottit.

VERSO 6

The seeds or spores of a fern are carried on the back of the leaf. Because a fern does not have a flower, sex occurs when rain falls and the spores fall to the ground and sprout and then some intricate and complicated thing that has taken millennia to develop happens.

At first the author thinks these pages will come in handy later. It's a benign enough thought. They're benign enough pages. Pages you can't use right now because the poem moved in another direction. Pages that are unformed, or pages that, at whatever moment, she did not have the patience or the reference to solidify. Or they are pages where the mind strayed: to a hopscotch box on asphalt; in Antigonish there was a fireplace; or that time in Escondido with Connie at the beach. The bar at the corner of the first street and the second street in San Pedro de Atacama where they played Black music, they said, on the board outside. The stranger, happy to see her for no reason at all. These stray thoughts might not serve a purpose. They're just like the dust under the bed where she used to go to read. Sometimes this dust would have an ant in it, or a spider, or a chrome green grasshopper caught by a spider. There from the stone in the front yard to the house, a continuous line of *Atta cephalotes* carrying cut bits of red ixora. There a substrata of life going on that people are unaware of. An abandoned web bereft of its chemical tensions. The broken pick of a guitar; certain streets she never visits anymore; a shout at 3 a.m. All this. What is in time? Radiation, the clerk says, seeing the wavy air of existence. The way things hover. The author hurries on her way to time's next accelerant foot.

VERSO 6.2

In Cuzco, a man coming from a wedding, the sun just gone down over the town's elevation. The man in one translucent gesture throws his dark wool poncho over his head; it descends to his shoulders, the garment settles, slowing time in one elegant gesture.

VERSO 6.3

Several questions the clerk has: from this angle, when will
we leave the body, the ribbed brace of human bones, the
whistling flutes of lungs at hemispheric windows and time
spent on the earth, the raucous coordinates of molecules
and who records their errors and their diatonic scales; here's
where what we do is listen, only listen to the blood and the
rowdy idioms of these cities jagging east, then west; this
submission to vastness that must be done at 6 a.m. each
day and 8 p.m. precisely; we dipped our hands in the well
of our chests to save ourselves, just this morning we made
our assignation with birds, to set our watches in motion the
coldest streets of several cities bellowed and disgorged their
pyrotechnic night-time parties; glide me across a wooden
floor as if in the arms of swifts in flight, sustain the chord of
G from one year to its nomadic next; of course we'll exist, I
suppose, but how, what would the world be with us fully in
it, what about the 900 petroglyphs of our embraces.

Controversy, against the turn, against the furrow

I finally joined the Communist Party of Canada when it
was almost at the end of its existence. Party meetings were
long bureaucratic procedures where many papers were read
and intense eyes directed at the people who had encyclo-
pedic brains full of Marx and history. I joined the artists.
There were artists of all kinds in the club, we were writers
and painters and actors, and there were even puppet
makers and comics. These meetings were possibly the
most boring meetings we ever attended. None of us ever
had a meeting perhaps to do anything that we did as
artists. There were photographers and musicians too and
proofreaders, and bookshop owners. And if we did have
meetings they would never be this dreary. The meetings
were deadly, tedious meetings discussing things I can't
remember now. I loved these meetings. There was a
conversation there that we never had to have about what
we were doing. In these muddy meetings there was a
clarity about our love. The same love as Lorca, and Neruda,
Saramago, and Carpentier.

A poet friend of mine, two in fact, who were not in the
party asked me once why I was a communist. I was taken
aback. I said, what else would I be? They stoned me with
Stalin. I pelted them with Sartre. I said I'm a communist
because I'm not a capitalist. They said this was simplistic.
I said yes, but it's clear. It was an evening in Massachusetts,
we were going to a reading, they said what had communism

done for Black people. I said what had capitalism done. They brought up pogroms. I brought up slavery. They said but you're Black, I said but you're Black too. They said these isms are only there to hoodwink Black people. I said most likely but I come from the working class. I had never thought of being anything else, for me it was simply logical, organic. One of them so annoyed with me asked, was I going to call Gromyko to ask him what I could say that night. I said, you call Reagan, I'll call Gromyko. We went silent and walked diagonally separated toward the reading. I read an erotic story about some teenage girls in love with their French-language mistress, this confirmed my shunning, we parted company, the diametric widened.

VERSO 8

Two enigmatic bales of pages arrived one day. The clerk
was adding up the countervailing duty as she usually did
on Mondays. Mondays because Sundays are a bad time for
the author. Just the sound of Billie Holiday alone accounts
for this. Eleanora Fagan can break any Sunday in two. So
this surprising Monday when the clerk had expected the
usual empty Monday of additions, two bales, one violet and
one blue, arrived. The blue was not like the blue of the
clerk's garment rather it was a blue like the blue off
Holdfast Bay on the Indian Ocean. The violet was inde-
scribable. How can you describe violet? It melts. There
were no consignee marks, except blue and violet.

VERSO 8.1

Violet rails, violet cancels, violet management, violet
maintenance, alizarin violet, the violet bale began. Blue
search, blue proceedings, blue diastole, blue traffic, the blue
bale began.

Lighter than usual, the blue clerk tried to figure out what to
make of these.

VERSO 9
To furrow, a row, a file, a line. Inventory

Some say that poets should not attempt it. Some. Some and
they. I absorb all the anxieties. But you don't resolve them.
You are no relief from them. You merely elaborate them.
You make me more anxious. How many times have you
said, it is not my job. I can do nothing about anything, the
clerk repeats. I can only collect.

Stay on matters of nature, on matters of love, on the
domestic, on language, sound. Furrow the same row. The
esoteric, not history, or politics. This is the conservative line
of poetry; to stay away from politics, stay away from
intervening in the everyday except soothe, sage, bring good
tidings, observe beauty; give light when all is dark; assure
us that we are benevolent and good at the core, lift us from
the daily troubles of the world, elevate our molecular
concerns, our parochial, individual lives to the level of art;
convince us that we are not petty and ridiculous; and
brutal, adds the clerk. And brutal, says the author. And
brutal, adds the clerk. That we are tied in to some universal
good, some deep knowing. The clerk sighs. That's god, or
mother, not poet. Listen to the bitterness dug into that
furrow. Poetry must be eternal not temporal. Who is at
eternity testing this theory?

The clerk is at the end of the wharf, the weather is as
aggressive as a metaphor. The metaphor, she's talking to
herself clearly, the metaphor is an aggressive attempt at
clarity not secrecy. The poem addresses the reader, it asks

the first question, it is not interested in the reader's comfort nor a narrative solution. It is not interested in your emotional expectations, or chronologies. It is flooded with the world. The great interrogation room is the stanza, you are standing at its door.

The clerk is at the end of the wharf, and the end . . . the weather is as torpid as a strophe. The strophe is a turning and a turning and a resolute turning. After, after, after the world is different. And after still, and after.

The grim list is presented by the clerk to the author, My inventory of war and democracy, she says. I'm Hecuba at the end of the Trojan War . . . *Lift thy head, unhappy lady, from the ground; thy neck upraise; this is Troy no more, . . . Though fortune change, endure thy lot; sail with the stream, . . . steer not thy barque of life against the tide. . . .*

I'm living in the world, the clerk shouts at the author. I'm talking about it next, the author insists. *What woe must I suppress, or what declare?*

I have an ink from cuttlefish; I have one from a burnt
pebble, one from several crushed juniper berries. This came
off in my hand. When did they arrive? They broke in.
Broke in where? Can't remember. When? Doesn't matter.
When are they leaving?

TWO

Elegy, the philosopher Gilles Deleuze remarked, *is one of the principal sources of poetry. It is the great complaint . . . the complaint is "what's happening to me overwhelms me." Not (simply) that I am in pain but what has taken away my power of action overwhelms me. And why do I see these things why do I know these things why must I endure seeing and knowing.*

To the leeward, the clerk replies, to the leeward, to the
northward, appears to be in ballast, wind is easterly
outside, made a signal of distress, ditto as the day before,
will not pass tonight, wanted a pilot, has a signal unknown,
squally and thick weather, sailed in the night, has drifted
out again . . .

The idea of an inventory, of overwhelming, came to me
since an inventory would be capacious enough to carry
what the poet knew or could know. An inventory is agape.
I need only open a new logbook, the items may be the
same or disparate, the only job is to list. That seemed the
least I could do given what I saw.

Inventory began one evening, sitting in front of the
television looking at the beginning of a war. A war, indefi-
nite article, warns the clerk, her finger rounding on the
back of *a*.

On the 20th of March 2003. The poem begins there but
I had been thinking for a long time about it. I was sitting in
my living room in a city of about five million people
observing a city of about five million people being bombed.
The menu on the television allowed me to watch this
program as well as others. And I am sure if I had looked
around I would have found on offer a romantic comedy or
two, a situation comedy or two, a rerun of *Law & Order*, a
rerun of *Seinfeld*, a nightly *David Letterman*, or the *Tonight
Show*, etc. . . . You could choose any of these entertainments.
Or I could choose the war. In other words, nothing stopped
for the war. In my city nothing was happening that caused
me immediate alarm. The street outside was lit in its usual
way; the neighbours weren't out there. Of course it was
March and cold, there was no noise that I recall not even
the customary siren calling from Lansdowne Avenue
where the drug trade took its usual shivering toll. Or perhaps

there was a siren but it had been years since that sound too had faded into ordinariness as the *Law & Order* reruns at least, had a perennial dramatic arc, a resolution, unlike the corner of Lansdowne and Bloor. The local social and political emergencies of poverty and drug addiction and their criminalizing had been cauterized by a welcome social distance; not to mention a home alarm system, a disaffection with the politicians, a lack of faith in justice, and the meme of otherness that dissected into atomic units of us and them. There is in our lives a televisual remove that one is afforded as a consumer of everything, a specta-tor of everything. The great spectator of the world. Nothing happens here, at least nothing that is not entertaining.

Will not pass the night the clerk mutters, wants a pilot,
requires assistance, not visible from signal station, made a
signal of distress . . . The clerk goes about indefinitely.

So I was sitting there on the edge of my chair with a
decision to make—pass on the war, spectacularly named
"Operation Iraqi Freedom" (the first episode was called
"Shock and Awe") or climb the stairs, go to sleep, and, as
with a tiresome baseball or basketball game, read the score
in the morning. It would be a blowout anyway. Like
watching the Raptors against the Lakers then. These are
the sickly enervating choices one is offered daily, living
where we live. And it is not that our days and nights are
not filled with the anxiety of finding a job, a place to live,
things to eat, dangers of violence, domestic and public, but
our lives are also filled with a comfort and certainty of the
truly catastrophic happening at a distance.

Unfortunately, not yet immune to the real-real, I sat and
watched with such anxiety, such nausea—it seemed/it was
immoral to rise and go to sleep.

The spectacle, of course, was for the grand spectator,
we, libidinous for disasters elsewhere, hate and pity is
what we find sexy. It was a light show of incendiary,
explosive ejaculations of bombs against the dark amorphous
cityscape that the commentators assured us was Baghdad.
All day before we had been seduced by an anemic map of
Iraq, its red corpuscles of towns and cities, missing—one
great star-like cell representing the goal of our desired
invasion/penetration. The real-real of that city lay secreted
from us. No one inhabited that place. We are accustomed
to this "no one" as you know, this "no one" is on our

ongoing colonial reality show. So, we did not see five million people prepare themselves, raiding grocery stores, filling up water, going to the bathroom nervously one hundred times that day, phoning family, and friends, hunkering down, biting their nails, looking their last time at gardens and bicycles, deserting neighbours in the cold immorality of thinking; in the end I'll have to take care of myself; becoming the source of suspicions, thinking too late of fleeing. Someone must stay awake, the clerk says, someone must dream them across the abysmal roads.

The commentators, our avatars with the maps, the excited voices, the graphic designs on their studio walls, they were us, included us, all we watchers in their "we" and their "us." We need not worry about "them," there was no "them." They did not exist—there was only a guy there named Saddam (now) (who had morphed, cinematically, into that other figure, bin Laden) who had to be apprehended along with his sons and his henchmen. A narrative we had ingested since childhood had to be enacted, so that we could enact it again. He wore a moustache, lived in a castle/palace, he was the obstacle between us and happiness; good and evil; he had weapons indescribably like ours. Look now how we were obliterating his city with them.

VERSO 10.3

At low water a red buoy, the western passage is the most
dangerous, care must be taken not to be swept by the tide.
Shows colours I can't distinguish, the clerk says, checking
her almanac of colours. Do, do, stock on deck. Transport.
Very far out.

One could not easily separate oneself from the "we"
constructed and being constructed by the spectacle and its
narrations or reiterations. And perhaps one ought not to be
able to so clearly distinguish oneself from that "we."
The grim list of the clerk begins, We believed in nothing,
the black-and-white American movies buried themselves in
our chests, liquid, glacial, acidic as love. The poet admits
culpability. This is not enough for the clerk. Don't let
yourself off, the clerk says, I have enough to deal with on
the wharf, thick weather, appears to be, easterly outside.
The clerk knows that admitting guilt is a cop-out, it's like
wanting to be noble without giving anything up, it is
drawing attention to yourself as if you are in a soap opera.
If the poet doesn't do more, the clerk will be inundated by
bundles of sheets tightly fastened with gnats and wire.

... because the author, she is a fiction in a certain reality, a spectre in a certain dream, a haunt in a certain night-mare. Since what I might be is uncontainable. The clerk of course understands this uncontainability, it is actually an extension of simplicity. I am so simple an idea, the clerk says, it is very complicated. We are working with some-thing that has already been concluded. It is not necessary to experience this body within the context of what is necessary in order to know it. It is conceived of before it appears or is investigated. I can never make such a mistake when I go through the blind shipment, the clerk says. That would be fatal. The author has heard this dissertation from the clerk about the freight, about the body, but is intrigued by the former sentence about the simple idea and its complication. When I say it is simple, the clerk knows the author's penchant for first sentences, I mean, it already exists, that definition, that place you are so eager to live in. Must I be explicit—the human—it exists in the world. But it is occupied.

The author is downcast, her instruments point toward the ground. But it is occupied by me, the author asserts helplessly. The clerk for all her vinegar cannot listen to this without pity. The author is standing at an estuary, the clerk sees, the tide is far out and the mouth of the river is dry. The thirty-six vertebrae of the author are about to fracture into dry pebbles.

The Clerk of the Versos scurries through the bales on

the wharf. She sweeps the gnats, disturbed from their indolence, aside. The wires come awake from the neighbouring bales. The one she is looking for came with no wires. She manages with great care to lift a page without rearranging its contents. The clerk's face must remain indelible for this task. This page is without verbs. It is a page she intends to give to the author as a kind of balm. This page has unstable magical powers of the same type the clerk believes, as say, the situation where poison is medicine. An antivenin. Without verbs nothing can be done, nothing can get in the bloodstream. There's lemongrass in it, if you like, there's bitter bark too, but the page is birdless and worldless, and there's a grand arithmetic and magnetic embryos and latitudes of where and where and here. Imagine the tenderness she must use, the held breath of the sea, the still dock, the tremulous bales alert, transfixed, the slight flap of the leaf, her watchful hand. Do you know the butchery it requires to skin the vocal tract for the soft, perfumed sliver of an *h*? The velar *k*, the bilabial *p*? Then, to circumlocute the corona of the tongue for *T* and *Th* and *S*? That is the clerk's job, and then, with the same professional alacrity of a slaughterer, to apprehend the constituting words and sift these for the unchastened perceptions, the incurable knowledges of who we are. The withholding pages, all their interests and their cynicisms, the volumetric capacity worries her. The clerk examines the useless curses, the stray sentences on why a life must be lived. She hurries back to the estuary and the disarticulating author. She lives in the accretion of the author's dreams.

The author lives on the aggregate of the clerk's senses. I am writing my way out of a nightmare, the author says. I am caught in a nightmare, the clerk says. Everyone knows how things get done in the world. The author is ready with excuses. The clerk turns to the author; the clerk's face is flooded with life. I don't, I don't know at all. I only know what a liquid consonant can do. The clerk is inclined not to trust the author with this page, but the page has its own poison or medicine. The verbless page leaves the clerk's fingers, floats down on the author's hand.

These versos began with three, then increased to seven, then elaborated to nine in the space of a few days. Now they are eleven. The left-hand page is not only chronic it is viral. The clerk retreats again to the wharf. Now they are fifty-nine.

The clerk is a misanthrope. She really has no faith or liking for people, not even for the author. The clerk thinks this is fine since she does not have to deal with people on the wharf. She is the only inhabitant, except for the insects and the dormant and dead plants. She is indifferent to animals, which is different from disliking them. Here at the wharf she does not get to see them since they are not necessary for delivery of the bales. The author drinks wine, talks of books, and animals, ever since she read John Berger's *Why Look at Animals*. To be fair, he confirmed the autonomy of animals for her. The amount of disassociation it takes to eat them. One time the author drank a whole bottle of champagne to boredom, bemoaning her life. This is the kind of person the author is, maudlin and self-pitying but basically a type of dishonest sybarite.

Blue tremors, blue position, blue suppuration. The clerk is considering blue havoc, blue thousands, blue shoulder, where these arrive from, blue expenses . . . The clerk hears humming in her ears; blue handling, she answers; any blue, she asks the author, any blue nails today? Did you send me, as I asked, blue ants? The author asks, blue drafts? Perhaps blue virus, blue traffic would make a sense, says the clerk, blue hinges, blue climbing, these would go together under normal circumstances. The author actually doesn't hear a thing the blue clerk says under these circumstances when the blue clerk sits in the blue clerk's place making the blue clerk's language. Systolic blue, any day it will be blue now, reloading blue, blue disciplines. The blue clerk would like a blue language or a lemon language or a violet language.

Blue arrivals. Oh yes.

"... and in the warped fantastic environment of our lives ...
For instance none of us had seen the outer world ... we were
the offspring of lovers convicts the poor and had been brought
to this forest by the Factory Committee ..."

KAMAU BRATHWAITE

It is here in the Black Angel that everything is said
already, everything that can be said. The author sighs.
How much you owe him! Quick radicles of green. And
more, green life and green balance. Terra verde. Alizarin
green. $CuCO_3(OH)$. Verdigris. That much green. The clerk
goes on. Black arrivals, oh yes, black valves of black
engines, black charges, black spins, black numbers,
black options, black equilibriums. Condensed smoke
of a luminous flame.

Now you owe him *the warped fantastic environment of
our lives.* And yes, the world I live in is not the world at all,
it is, if I ever look at it as a place, somewhere where the
years I manage to live will not be enough for me to live. I
will have spent the years I live in this warped, fantastic
environment of our lives.

Brathwaite. Black equilibrium Black spun.

Coltrane's "Venus" and the Ossuaries' *tercets*

In "Venus" there are two basic elements, the author paces,
the horn and the drums. They are working with double-
ness; they are working with time. There is one statement at
the beginning—the exordium—though this is not the
beginning, but the state of things. And then the instru-
ments proceed to deconstruct the statement in various
ways. The drum serves as pacing for the horn, but it has its
own investment in this state of things. It holds underneath,
but its own project is to also find deconstructions. The
drums, played by Rashied Ali, structure the horn and are in
turn structured by the horn. Coltrane works on the first
declarative syntactical unit. It is not declarative, the clerk
interjects, it is provisional, speculative, let us at least try to
be as precise as we can since. Fine, says the author, he
dissects that speculative, provisional statement, each sound
he breaks apart, technically. What is done becomes undone.
He also enumerates its emotion. If you listen to it, it is
romantic but mournful, sophisticated and worldly; it is
elegant. And he pulls these notions apart; he tears the
elegance to its limits, he rejects the mournfulness as
redundant and he drives the otherworldliness to its
outer-worldliness. To my way of seeing, says the clerk, it is
more elegant when it is, as you say, torn apart. So both
emotionally and structurally, the author continues, ignoring
the clerk's interruption (hearing it only as a faint sound at
her side), he pulls the statement apart. There's a point in the

middle, four or five minutes of it where the project takes hold of him, where the music is fully realized as separate and sentient on its own. There is an uncontrollability to it, and you can hear it wobbling out, out, out, into distances and into a kind of unspeakable. At least in your language, the clerk objects. And then the sound breaks and breaks and breaks. Around that point at about seven minutes the former statement tries to return, to recover itself, to recover the state of things, and it doesn't—so much structural and emotional change has already been accomplished. "Happened," you mean, says the clerk. So much has "happened," says the author, that the state, the register itself is now indescribable without its fragmentations. It rejects its former self, as well as it accepts that somehow that self like a shadow is embedded in it, in him. And what the drum is doing underneath, at that moment of complete disintegration, the drum sustains. Yet, yet, while the drum is attentive, the drum has disrupted its own discourse. "Venus" is like two travellers going out to an unknown. Not the unknown, says the clerk, they both have to pay attention, moving toward another, much more lucid, open state of being at the end.

To me, says the author, the tercets are like Rashied Ali's drums, consistent, sheltering, pushing; the three lines are completely steady. Though they never break from being three lines, they show that three lines can perform a range of acts of pacing. The tercet is conducting the ideas—the horn, the Ossuaries. You know nothing about musical

structure, the clerk says. But I can hear, the author says. I hear it as rhetoric. Liberatory. Then should I still be here on the dock, says the clerk rhetorically, shouldn't the ship have arrived, shouldn't this shoreline disappear. Instead, I need more burlap, more paper, more boards, more dunnage. More of everything.

The author ignores her again. The bitter-edged-ness, the global violence, one's own violence, the recognitions of one's own violence, the tercet anchors. Anchors, anchors, anchors, the tercet anchors. What colour is an anchor? The plunging clerk comes to catch her breath. What disrupts the tercet is the meaning. It is not regulated by rhyme or equi-metric length of line but by the sense of infinity or possibility, in-betweeness. It is indivisible by anything other than itself and one. The tercet is light, light as well as heavy. It can hold weight, as well as it can be sharp. It could be terse, and it could carry the weight of the ideas, and they could carry surprise. I might use them for a while longer, the author thinks, I don't know.

There isn't a full stop anywhere, they say. The clerk is only trying to get a rise out of the author. But what do you need a full stop for? You have the end of the line. The full stop is irrelevant. A full stop is really not even a point to discuss. Why discuss a full stop when you have a line? A line ends, and that is what that is.

What also happens is expansion and contraction. So, like with "Venus," there is this pursuit of a certain angle of the exordium, and then you go wherever that goes. But if I haven't said this already . . . You have said it, ad infinitum, mumbles the clerk . . . it changes where the line is enjambed, where it calls for attention, where the statement trips along giddily, or where it is full of weight. The tercet has guile. Like the body of a snake. Or on the other hand a triangle, or, less ambitious, the clerk joins, but more cunning, a bit of elastic. I could use a bit of elastic. The next time you come by. I would dye it blue like this paper. Only a snip bit of elastic, the clerk says. I would dye it indanthrene blue. But the author is drifting off.

Yes. And there is a mistake, the clerk says, a typographical one, somewhere there is a mistake. That is, a typo. I have it . . . But I just think those eight sustained minutes that "Venus" does is just so fantastic. You don't know when it begins, and it ends yes as you say, but it doesn't conclude.

THREE

The aphids move toward the light of these arriving pages. They do not make a wound, they leave no visible scar so you wonder why they are here on the dock. They land, they do not diminish. The blue light of the planet makes them rise, the yellow light of the young leaves makes them land. The clerk is a burning soul, she is attentive to the metaphysical survival of the stacks. She is a watching consciousness, her instincts are to survive, to order the bales, but not to "do" any more.

Except to leave. I think it is to leave. She would like a nice life, the kind she hears about on the right-hand page. That life the author is always dreaming on. The one where the clerk does not exist. I would like to be plain, the author says. But, the clerk rejoins, to continue to fight is to give up, it is to acknowledge that there are people who actually have a say in anything about your autonomy. To be plain requires so much work, you have to sandpaper all the viscera, and every branchial cleft.

The first bones emerged in the human zoos of the 18th century. 18th. . . . More like the 15th, the clerk says. Columbus arrived in Seville in 1493 with eight Taíno Amerindians kidnapped from Hispaniola. They become an adjective and lose their noun-ness.

I was reading that bit of paper when I noticed that I too lived in this modern zoo and re-enact each day a certain set of arguments, and suddenly being aware of the elaborate performances, I no longer wanted to have a part. They are horrendous. Those performances have used up generations of people, like a play being acted and re-enacted over time, the actors losing skin and bone, dying and being born again, inadvertently, to perform afresh these roles. All of my births and deaths. All of our births and deaths. On a spool. I leave my house and immediately my body is ripped from me to enact some colonial idyll. I look out a window. I wash my hands. I touch my eyebrows. I am on the eternal other stage. My teeth are examined. My arms are sized up. My hips measured. I pull my head in from the window. I try to hide. It's useless.

I am a watcher of the zoo, the author says. As well as a performer, this snide and dangerous clerk interjects. Even the language that we used to combat the more awful ailments, even that can be turned inward on itself. To *transgress* to *rebel*. They capitulate to the existence of a law, a *truth*. So you are dying in their etymology. And these words are, at the core, a construction of the zoo.

A dialect. Each word that seems perfectly legitimate right now, perfectly, as the vocabulary of what is called resistance, you will notice later only reinforces the zoo.

Essentially, as a poet. As anyone, the clerk says. As anyone, the author is trying her best to agree with the clerk this way life would be easier, so yes as anyone, you cannot be comfortable with any new arrangement. My job is to be completely uncomfortable, as painful and as horrible and sometimes as personally devastating as all that might be. You always have to distrust the comfort of solutions. It is incumbent upon me to keep being unsettled. Yet and still, the clerk thinks, you don't tell this to everyone, I alone see these versos and must bury them on this dock.

Back to Coltrane. Of course, you would like to go back to him, the clerk hums. Is it possible to reshape all kinds of understandings, and how would you do it?

It is very difficult to get rid of aphids; they do not yield
their leaves for soap and water as is commonly held. I have
tried. A ladybug is required. *Hippodammia convergens*. Or
green lacewing larvae. *Chrysopa rufilabris*. One ladybug
can, apparently, eat 5,000 aphids over its lifetime. A year or
so. It can also fly away. The clerk is thinking of sending
away for a pint of ladybugs. "Due to the perishable nature
of insects," reads the clerk, "we are unable to ship outside of
the continental USA." It is not clear where the clerk is, that
is, the clerk is not clear on her location. There is a dock,
there is an ocean, there might be a ship, there are bales full
of some urgency. But there is no address.

On hearing of my left-hand pages, ASJ, a poet, sent me this note from Edmond Jabès:

A book without room for the world would be / no book.
It would lack the most beautiful pages, / those on the left,
in which even the smallest / pebble is reflected.

Then I sent away for Jabès's book, *The Book of Questions*, and received it from England after some weeks. And there was his handwriting: *pour Jane et Sidney Shiff / j'ai été heureux / de connaître / En souvenir et / avec la cordiale pensée / d' E. Jabès.* This last note arrived with his cordial thoughts, says the clerk. Yes, so I suppose it is a sign that we continue, says the author.

I found this in Benjamin's *The Arcades Project.* On page 200. *Baudelaire . . . invites himself to absence. . . . he presents a new vision of his soul. It is tropical, African, black, enslaved.* Here is the true country, an actual Africa, an authentic Indies. It is from André Suarès's 1933 preface to Baudelaire's *Les Fleurs du mal.* What could it mean?

So the clerk searches Suarès' preface and finds more invective. He attacks Jeanne Duval, *She was the wheel of this Ixion, his torture, the barrel of Sisyphus with which he was burdened . . . alongside this black marble the man dreamt of the hot shadow of a mountain and of stifling Africa. She was a dumb beast. Unhappy, furthermore, neglected, avaricious, greedy, she drank and slept off her wine in the arms of the water porters. The drink took away her only virtue; silence . . . Baudelaire so fine and with such subtle sensibility, had this daily hell in his bedroom . . . etc., . . . etc., . . .* the clerk reads aloud.

So the clerk searched and searched *Les Fleurs du mal* for Baudelaire's tropical soul, his "African, black, enslaved" soul. I have searched and searched, she said, and I cannot find it. First I could not find the definition of such an object, neither the object itself, nor the manifestation of the object in Baudelaire. Except, except as a European aesthetic category. This must be what André Suarès was hammering on about in Baudelaire's poems. Could it be that Baudelaire ate the soul of Jeanne Duval? We don't believe in souls, says the clerk.

And Benjamin does he use the quotation to signify the

creation and commodification of this aesthetic? No. Though the work is about commodification in the end. And where are the zoos in *The Arcades Project?* There in the zoos, humanity is defined in the modern. Who is without, and who is within. Where that word is given more and more definition, and that definition looks more and more like a certain set of people and not like a certain set of other people, to the extent that those others are actually put in zoos. And how do they perform the body? They performed the animal; fossilized in spirit.

The clerk searches Benjamin and this is what the clerk finds in "Baudelaire" between pages 228 and 387 of *The Arcades Project*: viii references of references and notes to Jeanne Duval; vi of which call her by name; ii of which call her the consumptive Negress. They are as follows:

Jeanne Duval, Madame Sabatier, Marie Daubrun. [1]

If he loved in . . . a Jeanne Duval some immemorial stretch of night, . . . [2]

If Jeanne Duval played a part in the poet's emotional life analogous to that played by Aupick, we can understand why Baudelaire was . . . sexually possessed by her. [3]

Speak neither of opium nor of Jeanne Duval if you would criticize Les Fleurs du mal. *To conceive Baudelaire without recourse to biography—this is the fundamental object and final goal of our undertaking.* [4]

It should be remembered that Jeanne Duval was Baudelaire's first love. [5]

"L'Architecture secrete des Fleurs du mal." It represents an oft-repeated attempt to establish distinct cycles in the book, and consists essentially in the selection of poems inspired by Jeanne Duval. [6]

The consumptive Negress in Baudelaire. [7]

When he went to meet the consumptive Negress who lived in the city, Baudelaire saw a much truer aspect of the French colonial empire than did Dumas when he took a boat to Tunis. . . . [8]

Why make a verse of everything? And so what, says the author, what would be the interesting question there? Well, says the clerk, all the renovation of one thing and then another. Baudelaire, etc., . . . etc., . . . ? asks the author. Well, we know, replies the clerk, all the bitterness toward Duval and all the jealousies, but most of all the secret architecture of modernity. Of poetry, itself.

1 [J10, 3] i
2 [J14, 2] ii
3 [J17, 5] iii
4 [J19a, 3] iv
5 [J30, 8] v
6 [J37, 4] vi
7 [J51, 2] vii
8 [J54a, 7] viii

VERSO 16.2

Where is the medicine for this? The author's hand is at her
sternum. If I were some other substance I would cave like a
sandhill; an anthill.

10cc azurite

250cc amantine wole

26cc Peperomia pellucida grown in Amelia's garden, 1922

160cc yellow ochre levigated

alternatively

½ gr verdigris

50 gr poudre cloportes

30 gr poudre d'angusture / galipea officinalis

heat to 150 degrees Celsius

VERSO 16.2.1

I listened to the voice of Lola Kiepja, the Selk'nam shaman, as she moved toward all extinction. *Here I am singing,* she said. . . . *I have arrived at the great Mountain Range of the Heavens, the power of those who have died comes back to me, from infinity they have spoken to me. Here I am singing.*

VERSO 16.3
Museums and corpses

Here I am singing, the clerk said, I do not know, I do not
know how I have survived the world. I simply do not
know. I have such an ache in my back. All these laws so far
only ever address one arm, or one foot, over the long term;
they allocute one leg, one mouth; where one can sit, where
one can eat, where one can travel, and so on. They leave
me, perhaps, just one-legged and one-footed, one-armed,
sewing our vaginas, cursing the presence of our bare heads.

I do know that the bodies that we inhabit now are
corpses of the humanist narrative. Awful corpses. And,
when we appear on the street, that is what we are appearing
as. So, I can only give you this view of it. We inhabit these
bags of muscle and fat and bones that are utilized in
humanist narrative to demonstrate the incremental ethical
development of a certain subject whom is not we. We leave
the psychiatrist's office like the figure in Remedios Varo's
painting *Psicoanalista,* with a little container of our true
possible selves held out at arm's length in a plastic bag.

My job, it seems, is to notice, the clerk says. My job it
seems is to notice, the author says. Even as you are a living
object, you can make note, says the author. Look at the
display I am in the world, am I just that, you say. And you
can't sustain that double seeing for very long, the clerk
warns, otherwise, the body would truly collapse. The
19th-century human zoos; the schesis of human bodies. That
is when I left you, the clerk says, that is when I created you, 91

the author says, that is when I created you, the clerk says, that is when you left me, the author says.

It is a short step away, a short step away from the present. You are exaggerating and these exaggerations only pile up. I, I am exaggerating? the author asks. Look at the sky, the clerk beckons, look there is nothing else. You are living your life. Don't be naturalistic. Where is the great arctic, the endless dark days, the endless day-lit nights? However, if you were to stop for a minute and observe yourself, you are merely the container for a set of cultural knowledges and practices which go on without you, but which you are never without. They are like a bag of . . . a heavy bag on you. How do I get out of this zoo?

I can't position, I can't assure anyone of their ethical well-being.

Take this engine, the clerk says. You are living your electric life.

This organism that I am, I keep on going. But, we tend to think that as citizens . . . Don't be pompous, you're not a citizen of anything. Or . . . or . . . or . . . the author stutters. Or as constituted as communal, and citizen, and social, we tend to think of living as quite something more.

The author is not talking about a physical death, but the death of certain kind of spiritual, if you will . . . the death of a certain set of narratives, the death of the aesthetic of imperialism. It is an aesthetic that contains narratives of the body, bodies that the poet suggests were dead anyway. There are then ossuaries of these dead; of which my bones are some, the clerk says. We are some, the author says, yes, we are some.

The poet refuses to live in that world anymore, the world where certain bodies signify certain immovable qualities, deployed like lampposts along a route. To add yet another metaphor, the clerk sighs. What route is it and where does it lead then? So, it is the death of something completely useless, at least to the poet. Well, I can only give you a glimpse of these bits and pieces of a body that has been deconstructed as itself, and reconstructed as a set of practices in un-freedom. At least the poet, the author, well the poet is suddenly in a position where this fact is bare and raw and bald, and one may refuse habituation to it.

You have the privilege of this avant-garde seeing, the clerk says. It is not a privilege at all, to see, the author says. I think quite the opposite, to be the only person that this seeing is available to. The only person? Let us say then one of few. I don't think that is particularly avant-garde because people live that every day. Living that little fissure between scenes of the real. Everyone lives that everyday but we quickly seal the fissure for whatever pleasures are in the so-called reality, or, we give up on being on this side of the fissure because it is too lonely there. It is a chasm. It is a choice available to anyone, and apparent to everyone, but unfortunately, my job is . . . I wish I couldn't see that chasm. There's the pile of bones in that ossuary, where I threw the former poet. I think she is gone.

VERSO 16.4

Exactly.

"Well, it's much better now than it used to be," they say. But
I never used to be; I am now in the present, and what is
owed is owed. My entire life's energy is being placed . . . the
whole energy force of my human body is being placed at
the disposal of this enterprise of entering this enclosure.
I enter these rooms by these skewered methods, I ask for
whole humanity, they hand over my fingers; rearrange the
categories so that fingers are useless. I put my whole life's
work . . . into attending to the new assignments for entry.
The "I" that I am talking about is not me, of course . . .

VERSO 16.6

I am clinically aware. I am flying into light, that is, I am
flying west, flying into the recess of light, where light is
ending. I have taken each detail of myself apart and placed
them on the counter. These are the individual bits of
evidence. I expect an arrest to be made based on these
facts. Here is my heel, here is its classification. Who is in
detention except me? The commissioners and stenographers
must be notified, I said. Is there no one at the desk? What
will happen to my files? I am aware, always aware, clinically
aware.

If you say Foucault here, the clerk arrives brimming, you will be understood. By whom, says the author. By those you want to understand, says the clerk, though for me it is too late of course, but in your world. I am trying to find a language, yes, the author says, a language without . . . I am trying to find a thought, the clerk says, a thought without . . . a thought unburdened of all you are burdened with.

VERSO 16.8

I went, in other words, to all the commissions. I said, here is
my body, protect it. I said, arrest someone, immediately. I
would like you to issue a warrant. Here is my fingernail.
Send a team, a battalion if you can, arrest, seek out the
perpetrators. I have given you all the evidence. Here is my
signature. Nothing about me is false. I am surrendering my
body to you in whole. Someone must be charged with
murder. I said, why are you hesitating? I have surrendered
myself as I was advised. I am naked and have no visions.
Here I have signed the papers, you have my authority, such
as it is. The garments of glass, my shattered self. The
shatterings, I call them; my limbs, my ankles, my jaw.
Nothing here is missing. Someone is responsible. I went to
the quota of mornings. I said, here let us begin refreshed.
When will the charges be heard? I asked. I am still here
blue to the heels. I insist on my innocence, I am open like a
baby, I refuse cynicism on this.

I will wait all night, if it takes, for the report to be
handled. I can hardly disappear. The bailiff, with respect, is
one of them. So is the lawyer. I have brought myself as the
final forensic datum. It should be plain. Arrest someone.

I have now been here for quite some time. I no longer
know what language I speak or whether this one is the
original. I no longer exist, it seems, anywhere. Not this year.
I have been here each spring, ready to leave, certain of
what I can be certain of.

The dock is. The clerk thinks. Lemon summary, lemon factors. In the lemon distance are lemon wasps in lemon objections. Antipodal green, brindle marrow, marrow's satellite. What are you saying, the author says. Lemon hydrogen, the clerks thinks, insecticides. Lemon files.

We walked and walked and walked in Buenos Aires. At the MALBA you fell in love with Wifredo Lam for the eleventh time. We looked and looked as. You always forget him. I never do. Your love is like an annual plant. It dies down and has to be planted again.

Remembered, not planted. As soon as I see *La Lettre* I remember I love Wifredo Lam. The woman is standing with the letter. Her right hand covers her right eye, her left eye is closed, an aquamarine closedness. The letter is held against her body, it covers her right breast. She is nude. The letter is her temporary and secular clothing.

I think Jacob Lawrence had much more love in him than
you do. He had much more sympathy. When is he painting
them? He has much more hope, paintings so incredible,
incredibly riven with hope. He is painting them when he
thinks that that declaration might work, the clerk says. You
know, when am I writing this? Yes, the clerk answers,
quivering. I am writing this when nothing has worked, the
author says.

Lawrence puts all of people's ambition and all of their
solidarity into those paintings. In the painting *Coming
Home*, where there is one head, like an eggshell cracking,
and they are wounded, coming home, and it is so delicate
and so fragile, and what will they come home to? Of course,
after having joined their sense of the human with what
they thought was the universal, they come home to
penitentiaries, as I've said. Those paintings, they were a call
to the future, as much as Bird's *Ornithology*, later, or
Mingus's *Pithecanthropus Erectus*. A massive work, *Pithe-
canthropus Erectus*. These are all works about the human.
Each note has a political intent. In Mingus's liner notes, he
says, *Basically the composition can be divided into four
movements, evolution, superiority complex, decline and
destruction.* Mingus outlines the project as a dissertation on
hominid to human, he says, *Overcome with self esteem, he
goes out to rule the world, if not the universe, but both his own
failure to realize the inevitable emancipation of those he*

sought to enslave, and his greed in attempting to stand on a
false security, deny him not only the right of ever being a
man, but finally destroy him completely.

Mingus writes *Pithecanthropus Erectus,* and these notes, in 1956. There are no known translations that I can put my hand on, says the clerk. Hardly anybody reads it in that particular way, as a work of political philosophy. The clerk and the author have been scouring the existing libraries. But since the work departed like light it has not arrived in its future time, the clerk suspects. Someone, some future theorist might explain how we may absorb its philosophy despite our inability to read it in depth now. Maybe a future person will tease out or pull apart its meanings since our current capacities have yet to be developed to hear the full range let alone embrace its full meaning. Maybe we need a translator, the clerk says. I've only been able to make out the first two minutes of it like the first two chapters of *Capital* you are constantly going over. It is ten minutes and thirty-three seconds long, ten and a half volumes of a tome. It's a lot of work. The clerk is nervous. You aren't thinking of translating are you? These are arguments with history; these are arguments with reason, with the enlightenment. I just marvel at them and I wish I could do work like that.

Have you listened to *Pithecanthropus Erectus?* Amazing. Art is the only response to what we have been talking about. The only way not to engage the very kind of toxic imagination or what Cornelius Eady calls the brutal imagination, not to be hampered and weighed down by the toxicity of representation. It is too toxic, where we live, for any other kind of response. Every day you have to go into your house and detoxify, listen to, and translate one minute of *Pithecanthropus Erectus*.

Varanasi

Pilgrims have come to the golden temple, Kashi Vishwa-
nath, in the old city. I am there nearby and I am struck by
their seriousness. They have come to ask for something
from Shiva, and they have come to pay respect, and they
have flowers and are bathed in powders, their faces painted
in various decorations of the devoted. And I admire that
kind of devotion, as hopeless as I find it. You're such a
tourist, the clerk says, appalled. But I mean true, their
passion is true. And I understand totally that one gives
one's heart and belief to an unknown procedure. I'm sure
they're happy you understand, the clerk dismisses. Because
you asked me about Marx. So, pre-Marx, those are the
visions everywhere. This god, family, tribe. Post, maybe we
can imagine something else. We don't have to imagine
Marx's idea of the social either.

I hate your example. Why must you go all the way
there? I hate the context of your example.

A woman came toward me, glazed in belief. She was
incandescent with her faith; it shone on her skin. She
pushed me out of the path to the golden temple. She was
older, she was one hundred years with devotion. You're
jealous then, the clerk smiles for once. I still feel her
pushing my shoulder out of the way.

To each city I have travelled, I have only recorded the right-hand page. Delhi, and its traffic jams. On the way to Agra and all the towns in between, the camels on the highway; the women trailing saris on the backs of motorcycles; there's a photo of you there in Fatehpur Sikri. In Kochi; the dhobi wallahs up to their knees in water and soap and the brief brown post office resembling the one where I was born with my grandfather accounting for seas. All the right-hand page. I never saw the left. Naturally, says the clerk. What it is to see what everyone else sees before they even arrive. That is easy enough. Not even in Vietnam or Cambodia, though there were times. That time, you sent yourself a postcard from Ho Chi Minh City, remember? You wrote, *Hi d, Love always. D.* You put three stamps on the envelope, the card was a drawing of three women riding bicycles. I have it, you may be sure. And when you returned home you read your note and it surprised you how raw "Love always" sounded. And you could not enter the rooms at Tuol Sleng, you said the people were still there, even now the hairs on your body rise with alert as when you stood there unable to enter. I've filed all of this for what it is worth, what you put down is only on the right-hand page. Just as I've kept the thousand people you tried to share a sunrise with at a famous temple and mercifully the sun did not rise since no one would have seen it. No one was interested in seeing the sun rise, you said, they were only interested in taking a photo of the sun rising.

Why did you visit these sites of terror? I went to visit the
world. I went to visit the years of solidarity with the world I
was in solidarity with. I had read thousands of newspapers,
I had followed the arguments, I had chosen sides. I had
lived through, like someone on the other side of a
telephone line, all the events, all the events had shaped me
though they had not happened to me in the same way as
they had happened to the speaker on the other end of the
telephone. I therefore visited to say to the air and the
bodies, to the electrical wires—Here I am, I was on the
other end of the telephone during all those years. I expected
to find exhaustion, since how we live here is to use up
those bodies there, give them a constant pounding and
reworking and very often kill them. Instead I saw with
relief, one million motorcycles in Ho Chi Minh City with
two million young people riding them. That is when I sent
the postcard to myself.

Blue the clerk has collected from exhaustion: blue maxi-
mums, blue wine, blue safety, blue descent, blue crossroads,
blue havoc, blue marrow, blue speed, blue shoulder, blue
appliance, blue heavy, blue balance, blue nails, blue injector,
blue steering, blue mileage, blue handling, blue tremor, blue
watches, blue clippers, blue corks, blue apples, blue positions,
blue crimes, blue catheter, blue sprinkle, blue expenses, blue
opportunities, blue discriminations, blue disciplines, blue
suppuration, blue ants, blue proceedings, blue traffic, blue
increases, blue hinges, blue request, blue any day, blue
version, blue decline, blue draft, blue sleep, blue calling, blue
gentile, intended blue, blue search, blue reload, blue virus,
blue edge, blue starch, blue protein, blue density, blue
fingerprints, blue nibbed, blue climbing, blue ditches, blue
quarrel, systolic blue, blue maintenance, blue hold, blue
number, blue drama, blue sustenance, blue edge, blue
percent, blue indent, blue itself, blue schemes, blue file, blue
lagan, blue rain, rind blue, blue turbine, blue visas, blue
filled, blue tolls, blue storage, blue help, blue sex, poised blue

Violet the clerk has collected: violet hand, violet notes,
violet coolness, violet edging, violet halls, violet finger,
violet region, violet fuel, violet metre, violet breath, violet
written, violet hatreds, violet hammer, violet bed, violet
wires, violet arms, violet apples, violet digits, violet washes,
violet thyme, violet dialysis, violet records, violet scissors,
violet palms, violet onion, violet speed, violet construction,
violet fog, violet lane, violet yield, dry violet, half ton violet,
cord violet, violet management, violet sleep, written violet,
hung violet, violet suspension, violet carburetor, violet
labour, violet genocide, violet mud, violet lizards, violet
chemical fences, violet chill, violet intended, violet taken,
violet ambulances, violet incarceration, violet shoving, violet
February, violet field, violet episode, violet rails, violet reply,
violet brassiness, violet blind, violet brick, violet cancels,
violet spite, violet profession, violet shame, violet limb,
violet smoke, violet chest, violet rains, violet jars, violet pays,
violet haunch, violet sticks, violet coast, violet vein, violet
teeth, violet gorse, violet escarpment, violet hoarfrost, violet
museum, violet rues, violet recovery, violet creek, violet
carpool, violet requirement, violet plans, violet openings,
violet empties, violet asylum, violet criminal, violet angers,
violet manuscripts, violet introduction, violet terminals,
violet maintenance, violet fame, violet probations, violet
hours, violet snares, violet whimper, violet officials, ample
violet, violet chained, better violet, same violet, violet xray,
violet becomes, hidden violet, violet blunder, violet early,

missed violet, violet itself, violet prescription, scabrous
violet, violet thumbs, violet belief, violet riot, never violet,
violet spur, intended violet, pinned violet, violet respiration,
violet staples, day violet, exhausted violet, greyed violet,
opening violet, violet gravity, violet help

Lemon the clerk has collected: watch lemon, bay lemon,
rare lemon, lemon distance, lemon steps, given lemon,
lemon knot, lemon reach, lemon fast, lemon documents,
lemon ethic, lemon funerals, lemon hold, taken lemon,
lemon elegies, lemon summary, lemon pulley, lemon
factors, lemon archives, what lemon, lemon acts, lemon
nails, lemon steps, lemon crevasses, written lemon, lemon
vanishing, lemon deposit, missing lemon, lemon contents,
lemon debris, lemon gains, unassailed lemon, lemon sinew,
uncertain lemon

Poema, poein, related to, the Sanskrit, cinoti, cayati, to
assemble to heap up, to construct

I can't do everything. That is what someone assured me.
She said, "You can't be responsible for remembering
everything." But those are strange things to forget. Like
coleus? No, like your fingers. Well of course one forgets
one's fingers. They simply do what they do. I suspect other
motives, the clerk stabs.

Poetry can expose the heterogeneous qualities of a life,
or of life, in an age in which all efforts both corporate and
State, seem to homogenize. I think that poetry has the
capacity to blow oxygen on a stiff existence, right? Jesus,
the clerk says. I mean, I'm saying that, but if you think of all
the mechanisms of communication and all the availability
of information, you're thinking, well, that's not particularly
homogenous or that's not particularly stiff, or needing of a
type of oxygenation. But, not true, the clerk interjects. I
think it is stiff, because it is a repetition of the same thing,
over and over and over again. All the information about
what a life might be, what a life might look like, how a life
ought to be lived, what one must want and desire, all those
roads are quite flattened out into certain needs and certain
tastes and certain wants. And that person, the author says,
that human, has now become fairly describable, as some-
one who is striving not to think too deeply about very
much. All information is available, all history is available,
all thought is available. Consuming is the obvious answer

to life. This availability exists, the clerk says, but it really exists in the brain; it doesn't exist in the mind. One is rushing over it, or one has a landscape, but it isn't a lived landscape, all the details aren't lived. I'm not sure where that was going, the clerk trails off.

A line of poetry does about five things, whereas a line of prose can do five things, but it has a full stop. You seem obsessed by the full stop, the clerk has beckoned with her dry hand, why not just leave it out of the novel. I think the imperative, in a certain sense, for prose to satisfy narratively makes prose unavailable to the generative possibilities that a poem has. You have never been able to articulate this well or convincingly, the clerk insinuates. Each time you attempt it, I end up with this incoherence and this uncertainty. The clerk sighs to a thousand files, they groan with a sweep of her hand. I can think of hundreds of novels that contradict you. A baby was born next door, the clerk continues, as if we are talking about the same subject. I'm thinking about making him my assistant.

It is not that prose can't do it . . . I am being careful here because as you say there are many, many works . . . I have written prose, and I know that it is possible to perform these generative moves, these imaginative . . . the author incoheres, . . . all those moves in it, but essentially, you still owe something to the reader, you know, understanding, in ways that in poetry, you don't owe them at all. It is a negotiation between what is said, what is written, and what is withheld. And you are always balancing this, so, if prose is on the continuum between what is written and what is withheld, it would be, perhaps, somewhere in the middle, and poetry would be three-quarters of the way along that line in terms of the possibilities of its withholding, and the possibilities of its revealing. What was the question again? I can't remember.

Poetry has that ability to reconstitute language; it uses time. It can make you see the xylem between the then and the after, or the now and the after. It has no obligation to the present. It *is* time.

A buoy has been placed outside a grap of rock about one
and three-quarter miles from shore, in three fathoms of
water. Mariners should not go south of this.

The following are the usual rate of freights.

Josephine Turalba has made me a pair of slippers. They are
my favourite colour, and gold. They are elegant with
violence, as elegant as violence. They are bullet-ridden and
elegant. They are bullet-made and elegant. And fine with
violence, as *violence* is the only word I know for elegance.
They are perfect and contain all the violence in the world.

Adjectiveless, the clerk thinks, balance, daily, no qualification, ink perhaps, sincerely. Dear. File 65. Attempt 197. The clerk needs a spanner, a vehicle, a bowl of nails, a wire, a cup, a lamp. A lamp? Bring file 267. Attempt 501. Handles.

Alice B. Toklas on Gertrude Stein on Picasso on Gertrude Stein: *In these early days . . . the effect of the african art was purely upon his vision and his forms, his imagination remained purely spanish. . . . She was not at any time interested in african sculpture. She always says that she liked it well enough but that it has nothing to do with europeans, that it lacks naïveté, that it is very ancient, very narrow, very sophisticated but lacks the elegance of the Egyptian sculpture from which it is derived. She says that as an American she likes primitive things to be more savage.*

Who on earth is left who did not say an awful thing, the clerk wonders. Who. Who did not disguise it as sophistication, as knowledge, as wit. What jaded poses dismiss all dreadfulness. How the author bears all this is alarming. And that isn't even the worst. Such memory loss you have. *Melanctha.* My amnesia is useful. How many micro-abrasions, as they say, do you think I could take?

Rose Johnson was careless and was lazy, but she had been brought up by white folks and she needed decent comfort. Her white training had only made for habits, not for nature. Rose had the simple, promiscuous immorality of the black people. Rose Johnson and Melanctha Herbert like many of the twos with women were a curious pair to be such friends. Melanctha Herbert was a graceful, pale yellow, intelligent, attractive negress. She had not been raised like Rose by white folks but then she had been half made with real white blood.

Each sentence is a razor blade. Toklas says (and still I am honouring the conceit) ... And still you are honouring the conceit. Can you call it a conceit anymore, truly? You're right of course but Alice says that when Gertrude Stein wrote this it was *the first definite step away from the nineteenth century and into the twentieth century in literature.* Well all that is certainly generous, the clerk laughs. Sometimes the clerk laughs an uncontainable laugh. An unruly, veering laugh. It veers and it cracks and the author hears it like a bone being broken when a car hits it out of the blue. And even so, the author quotes Alice B. Toklas, *Gertrude Stein concluded that negroes were not suffering from persecution, they were suffering from nothingness. She always contends that the African is not primitive, he has a very ancient culture and there it remains. Consequently nothing does or can happen.*

Didn't Hegel say that? It's all I remember of Hegel. The clerk is laughing now like machines cutting gravel in a quarry. See Picasso's *Acrobat and Young Harlequin,* 1905. Just to state the obvious, the clerk states the obvious. These effete and childish paintings, their organ-grinding stupidity. Then observe the utter ripping of Picasso's sensibilities, the shredding of his senses when the African sculptures entered him. Then, *Head of a Woman,* 1907. *Head of a Man,.* 1907. The author and the clerk mimic Alice with their hostile pity, ... *the charming early Italian period to the intensive struggle which was to end in cubism.*

Is there an essentialism creeping in here. The tentative author. No, a tiredness with having to recuperate, from essentialism, the conversations going on in the African sculptures so they may go on their way. In a future uninterrupted they break their own mythologies. Will I? The plaintive author. Who knows.

Mourning cloak seen out the window, it moved from the smoke bush to the late cherry tree to the wisteria and then the grape leaves. A possible roadway, the clerk observes.

VERSO 20.01

Any clerk who in any vessel lying within twenty yards or alongside who makes use of any violent or obscene or profane language with intent to provoke any person, fights, or disturbs the peace shall be guilty of a contravention of these regulations.

I have seen Apollinaire's things. The twenty-four African
sculptures. *C'est par une grand audace du goût que l'on est
venu a considérer ces idoles nègre comme de véritables
œuvres d'art.* The Fang, the Kuta, the Baule . . . C'est par
une grand impuissance du goût que l'on n'est pas venu a
considérer ces sculptures africains comme de véritables
œuvres d'art.

I have nothing to say about God. All of those kinds of philosophies got us to this place. I don't know where women exist in those religions, they are absent in those visions. They do not exist. Or, they exist as something called "women." But they certainly don't exist as something called "human" or sovereign. So, I find religions useless. I don't want to ever have to defend them. Not much more to be said there. If my friends come to me and say, I have a right to pray, I say of course you do, pray but do not involve me. Do not involve me in your wretchedness. I do not need forgiveness and I do not need salvation and I do not need excuses and I do not need denigration or elevation. And most of all I resent your assignments, and most of all I resent your cowardice and your violence.

Let us be honest, women never talk directly to god.

Mourning cloak. Black with yellow border. *Nymphalis antiopa.* Antiopa, people have no idea the effects they have on other people. *Nymphalis antiopa,* everything shatters, everything breaks to the touch. The green birth of the wisteria the author watches a spring long, the hapless sparrows.

VERSO 21
Xylem

Reading Jacques Roumain . . . there is newness, there is an
incredible newness of ideas and thoughts, because that is
the challenge. I mean, I think that space is . . . I am going to
follow Wilson Harris on that . . . Ellison is the only one
who has written a book entirely of left-hand pages.

You can't really say that Gabriel García Márquez is a
Colombian writer. He is from Colombia, but as you read the
work, the work expands way beyond this border. So he is also
from everywhere else. No one notices? No one notices the
cultural policing. The work that is produced and why, and in
relation to what. It is always in relation to itself. What are you
saying, says the clerk, of course it is in relation to itself. No,
I mean to a very finite self, formulaic: marching to itself as
the perfect society. And post the towers an even more finite
self. There is absolute censorship. Some of us were always
censored. A triangular trade of censorship, the clerk giggles.

Marsalis, his jazz project . . . these are efficiencies,
rationalizations, and we can't fault them. How did we get to
Marsalis? All are in relation. To continue, we must under-
stand them as a kind of rationalization into nation. He has
become an accountant, reminding them of the tally. The
clerk is alert to the tables of weights and measures. The risk
of not doing this accounting is to exit the discussion, to
take your leave. The risk of accounting is to forfeit a bigger
discussion, a bigger life. But you understand the impulse
and the impetus, asks the author. I feel sad sometimes for
him. He is wearing himself out doing this accounting; his
own art is dormant. Let me remind you of your earlier
dissertation of the aesthetic of imperialism, all our art is
dormant, archival, fiduciary. Not about existence. I suppose
he must have a clerk like you. I would hate to meet his
clerk if you are any example. And I would hate to meet
Marsalis himself, if you are any example.

VERSO 21.2

The clerk understands that this wooden dock is attached to nothing; no land, no town, no city. She notices the bryozoa colonies growing on the joists. Their starburst cilia waving, their gelatinous rooms expanding.

Two, the clerk has said to the author, two people down to themselves is not sufficient. Then there is really only one. But really the clerk is solitary.

Measures of surface, measures of weight, measures of solidity and capacity, fluid measure. High water and variation.

VERSO 21.3.1

The piece of art that they send to the future both spoke
and didn't speak of that place that they lived in, that
particular local moment that they lived in. How to make
tracing paper out of paper according to Cennini. How to
tint paper . . . What are you reading. Some instructions to
leaping beyond the time that we live in, or, natural blue he
says exists in and around the vein of silver . . .

My grandmother used to say you should wear a maljo
blue near to your chest to ward off whatever.

Ellison is the only one who has written a book entirely of
left-hand pages. First, his clerk (we are acquainted) lived
underground and selected many pages sent above. They
arrived as he had written them from the world of the
unseeable. They have been, as you would imagine, misread
as in due course these versos will be. The protagonist lived
in a world, as I, of the absurd, but somehow everyone
believed it was credible. Just summon Baudrillard here if
you like. The hyperreal was hyperreal already. For us. The
protagonist lived as an avatar, a projected image. He
performed some tasks, and sometimes in the book you can
see how paper-thin the world is he is trapped in, as in the
paint factory. Or, at the party meeting. Or, on the street
with the marionette. There is a way of reading it all as if it
were only of its own time, as if the protagonist is of that
time; to read the crude regime that repressed the protago-
nist's body as a morally legitimate space into which the
protagonist desires entry is wrong. The more significant
reading is that Ellison, like his clerk, was beyond time.
Ellison wants us to take note of the repressive machine and
its evacuating of the protagonist's body and will. The book's
absurdism is entirely lost as the regime's legitimation
processes latches it to the conformism it jumps out of. This
dock is my dock as the room of light is his. There were
thousands of pages remaining of his left-hand pages.
Ellison's clerk and the author had many thousands of hours
of debate and in the end they retained all those documents.
After his death of course these documents were discovered
and assembled erroneously, since the regime still exists.

Harris. *Palace of the Peacock.* Another document. Every
sentence ends in a paradox. But how do you read Donne
climbing up to the palace. This way. I hope Donne never
rises. Is never "I." It is Donne who must become human.
Donne dies in the beginning. Killed by Mariella. And is
hung. And drowns. I.

I want to agree about what Harris calls the "unfinished
genesis of the imagination"; "involuntary association"
though is trickier to make stand still.

"A bias grows," he says. Yes, . . . *A bias grows which may
profit from that hidden relationship in purely formal
experimentation (Picasso's formal, let us say, appropriation
of facets in the African mask); but unless a genuine cross-
cultural apprehension occurs of the unfinished genesis of
the imagination affecting past and present civilizations,
an innermost apprehension of changing, cross-cultural
content within frames we take for granted, the involuntary
ground of association . . . remains between privileged and
afflicted cultures.*

There is the problem of course. Harris is hopeful. Why
must you be so pessimistic? Well, I have had some time,
you know, and an angle. Time has eaten me away. The
hidden relationship? Yes. Look, if you want to, at my sides.
And my toes. The sighs of the clerk whistle through the
wood of her.

VERSO 22
Latifolius—broadleaved

This is the truth. The clerk bows her head at this weary
subject. She hears the prevarication in that direct object.
I lose a lover every ten years or so. I don't know how.
Another sigh strafes the blue robes of the clerk. Her eyes
become dim diamonds. I don't know how.

I went to the Museum of London Docklands on the
West India Quay. There on the wall there were lists of ships
and their cargo during the trade. I was startled to see a
name. John Brand, he was the captain of a ship named the
Mentor, owned by William Lyttelton, and on April 5, 1792,
it loaded up in the Gambia with 141 people whom it took
as slaves to Dominica. On this wall at the museum there
were recorded three more journeys of the *Mentor* captained
by John Brand to the Gambia.

When the clerk receives this she asks the author, But
this is perfectly respectable for the right-hand page. Why
burden me with this too? Yes, the author said, but it is so
tedious, this type of material is worn out yet it keeps flying
around like love flies around in the head, so much debris,
brain debris, like the memory of lovers or wives. It repeats
without resolution. No one wants to hear about it anymore,
but it stays in the air. I wake up and it's there, I go to sleep
and it's there, I look out on the garden and it is there. It's
invisible like the debris around our planet now but it's
there, emitting shafts of pink and green light through
the atmosphere.

Light? the clerk remarks. I have changing weather, massive storms of many kinds, changeable in any minute. You have loves, you have wives? The clerk thinks about this for a moment. The clerk would like to have loves, would like to have wives, perhaps a bare house near the wharf, with a lantern for the evenings, a kerosene lantern with a round filament that puffs and lights when the lantern is pumped. Also a coal pot with a platein from which the smell of unleavened bread would rise; and a book with no writing in it, simply blank pages that the clerk might read and laugh with. She submits her weathered shoes and her inky hand, her tattered hem.

I've looked for that John Brand but only found another who could and could not be the same; this one was a clergyman and a writer born in Norwich and died in 1808. He wrote a pamphlet called, "Conscience, an ethical essay." I cannot find that. The essay or the subject. It would be perfectly normal to write such an essay, whose contents I can only imagine, and still steer a ship to the Gambia, pick up 141 people, and transport them, tethered, to Dominica, returning the profit to Baron Lyttelton. Three times. Three voyages undertaken by John Brand. Yet this could not be he. This John Brand took up a position at the rectory of St. George's in Southwark in 1797.

It's only by chance that you found that on the wall of the sugar museum, you weren't looking, the clerk admonishes, you must be more careful with this collecting of yours. Such an encounter only brings more grief than you can handle. At first with you it is wonder and then it turns into grief, just like your wives. Apparently John Brand was a writer and an antiquarian as well as a reverend; he published a poem, "On illicit love. Written among the ruins of Godstow nunnery, near Oxford" (1775). You have a lot in common then, the clerk said, going too far.

There was a Thomas Brand, a Whig, who was in the British Parliament at the same time as a William Lyttleton, this Lyttleton was also a Whig and according to *The History of Parliament* was "listed among the 'staunch friends' of the abolition of the slave trade, the subject of his second speech, 16 Mar. 1807."

Well they would have made their money by then, I suppose, time to launder it in democracy. At any rate, at the moment I can do nothing about this, I need a historian. Because at this point it is ephemera.

I wish this would be over so I can get on with my life, the author says. How long do these centuries last.

As a footnote, hectors the clerk, in 1780 Robbie Burns was on his way to Jamaica to be a bookkeeper on a slave plantation. He published the Kilmarnock edition to sell and to collect funds to enable him to make the voyage. If not for its success . . .

Why are you telling me of this? the author asks. Just to remind you that . . . it is possible that everything is washed in it.

Strophe, turning from one side to the other of the orchestra,
the act of turning

I would like, therefore, to live in time and not in space. Not
the timelessness that is often spoken about but time, in this
world, as if living in an area just adjacent to air, a film of air
which carries time and where I could be in several imper-
sonations of myself, several but simultaneous. If there were
time like this.

But there is time like this. A pause from the author. The
clerk lives in time like this, several and simultaneous. The
author lives in place and not in time. Weighted. In place.
I am always aware of myself in place. There is no universal
me. I am specific. I am the critique of the universal, we live
distances apart. We negate each other.

VERSO 0.1.2

I walked into a paragraph a long time ago and never emerged from it.

"'The house I was living in when I read that book,' you think, or 'This colour reminds me of that book.'"

Rhys? Yes.

At this point the clerk lay down, her hands on her face. The sea rolled in, in its usual way, as if a ship were imminent. The clerk dreamed for a moment of when she was nineteen or so, when all the things that happened to her happened in a feverish way. In this dream she felt a contraction of her heart at the thought that if she'd never arrived at the dock, the randomness of life would have enveloped her. Much as the dock was the burden of things, much as the dock's great load weighed her down, she had arrived, intentionally and with something like freedom, with a satchel of air with a clasp on it.

Each scene of the clerk's life before replayed itself and she felt the hair on her arms prickle with fear. Suppose she had stayed at the telephone company on the night shift listening to conversations on the lines? About marriages, about babies, about someone stabbed in a parking lot with a pair of scissors, about long-distance love affairs between Minas Gerais and Oakwood Avenue. Suppose the boyfriend who slapped her and left her without her clothes in a motel had still been her lover? He worked in a plastic-making factory and eventually had his shoulder broken by the mafia, not for leaving her naked in the dim room in winter but for something else. Suppose desire in this kind of drama had never suddenly, one day in the middle of a cricket match at a savannah, become bald and disingenuous? Suppose she had not awakened one night to the curtain moving with something more than the wind, and the door

137

sliding open in the living room and surprised the man who
had tried to surprise her with a sound from her throat half
bellow, half scream.

And the bus, driving toward the other possible life.
There is always a bus driving toward another possible life.

The clerk shivered and waking looked at the ocean. Still
as an inkwell. The dock was solid, the atmosphere slightly
dry, a faint smell of smoke. The clerk sets off on her
inspections. These bales try to set fire to themselves and
that would be fine if it could be done but all they do is
smoulder.

VERSO 24

You cannot live the same life as you imagine. You must live a smaller life, a more compact life. The life you imagine is too capacious, you will lose your balance. Driving home, I think this.

VERSO 24.1

Sometimes I am overloaded, too many people, too many thoughts, the author says. And these thoughts, these desires, are insensible anyway. A waiting room at the driver's licence office is the worst place to be when you feel overloaded. Waiting rooms are, in general, places of suffering, of kneeling to bureaucracy.

From the malls, the author has brought the clerk many
stories. There are people, she says, who have cut off whole
parts of themselves to acquire the elusive perfection that
this city needs. There are people who have become quite
ugly in finding that perfection. There is no delicate centre
to them, just the coarse exterior of getting and wanting.
Maybe they save that delicate interior for when they're at
home alone but in public all that's on display is that violent
wanting, the author adds.

    This is how the author would put it. I hate malls. They
fill me with revulsion and hatred for everything.

The author thinks that she is invisible, the clerk thinks. She thinks she has the right political distance. Of course I recognize that when the author's name is called to go for her road test, her second road test, I will once again be dragged into the maelstrom of her social world. Everything is regulated, the author says, everything, and one cannot simply live as one wishes driving around the city with no sanction from the authorities—and even one's most private thoughts are regulated by announcements everywhere and police stopping you for what they ridiculously call a rolling stop and then asking for your licence to drive. The man across from the author is looking at her intently and she wonders if by chance some thought of hers has escaped and is floating around her head like a halo. The author meets his stare. Then he looks at her shins and the author looks at her shins covered in her best pajamas, and it takes her a moment to grasp his disapproval and she looks at him with pity. How sad she says to the clerk. He has allowed himself to accept, rather, to be battered into some norm he expects me to observe. I can see his left cortex smashed in with this idea. "Your head!" she says aloud in his direction and the man inclines his head a degree in her direction but not his eyes. She thinks to say more, like, "What fucking business is it of yours how I'm dressed." Or perhaps, "Don't panic guy, I'm sure this room is full of women you'd approve of so don't let it drive you crazy." But then she thinks, that is precisely it, it does not matter how many people conform. It is the non-conformists who must be rooted out and who must be policed. The guy, to be truthful, looks like a common enough guy, the clerk thinks, like a guy on a tight lunch hour but the author won't leave it alone because it is precisely this situation, precisely this kind of guy who is an enforcer for the powers of regulation. It is this enforcer sitting here casually, quite casually, who carries out the daily work of bringing people like me into line. The man remains unmoved by the author's thoughts. The clerk thinks of getting up and stepping toward him before the author does. Try to control your temper. Why should he commandeer the waiting room of the licence office with his violence, the author has lost control. The clerk gestures around the room and the author becomes aware of a phalanx of enforcers all sitting strategically with the same broken skulls, the left cortex smashed in, their bodies all concentrated in surveillance poses. So when the clerk's name is called and the examiner turns out to be one of these guys, the author rises and makes for the door.

In the mornings the clerk reads the obituaries. All these bales may be considered obituaries of a sort but we are talking about the regular obituaries where people actually die. Here on the dock nothing and no one dies. The clerk would like them to die the finite closed death of a real obituary of the type as the ones in newspapers. Aphids do not kill leaves, per se. They extrude the sap of them and they expel a sweet substance of their own called honeydew, etc., etc., on down the line.

It came back to her this morning. She was running in a
relay. She was twelve and there was a pain in her ankle
bone, it ripped from the heel right up to the ankle bone
and she almost stopped running but she was the last leg of
the relay and her friends were waiting at the finish line.
Patsy Sones had fallen in the third leg so the clerk was far
behind already. And then the ankle started to hurt but she
said to herself, "No. I am running." And then someone said
to her, "Hmm." And she almost stopped running. And this
someone, who she was to notice all her life, said, "Hmm,"
again as if expecting failure. And she swung her head
around risking being totally left behind to see who was
talking to her but there was no one. And she thought the
voice must be inside of her head, but she thought about it
and it wasn't. It was right at her eardrum, not inside her,
very definitely not inside her. And just like that she had a
glimpse of her future self and that is who it was saying,
"Hmm." A future self, drinking a beer in a neighbourhood
bar with a cross look on her face. A future self who didn't
say any words, just hmm, like that, lifting the beer to her
lips and squinting at the sun through the plate-glass
windows with a red painted sign. Imagine having a voice
like that say hmm at your school track meet when you're
twelve. Imagine how early that voice appears, and imagine
that you don't really understand that tone, that sly interrup-
tion. And when all you are doing is trying to recover your
House dignity because Patsy Sones fell and was late getting
the baton to you and you already had to stand and wait

while all the other girls ran ahead of you. But small as she was she tried to ignore it, that voice which sounded older and which was like a voice from the definite future and was taking advantage of her. But even then the clerk had the will to ignore that voice. She ran and she ran. She picked her legs up and she ignored that little pain and she came in second. She was disappointed. Especially with the voice behind her, next to her ear still saying hmm. Like a sentence, like something it knew about her already, and not like a warning or anything, not like something saying slow down or speed up, but like something with a forever prediction. How hard it was to outrun that voice. But the clerk did outrun it and her mates were waiting for her at the finish line, even though she only came second. And they grabbed her up and spun her around and Patsy Sones looked so absolutely grateful as if she owed the clerk for the rest of her life. The girls screamed, "We came second!!" As if they had come first.

And so the voice saying hmm receded in this screaming but of course it never quite went away the clerk now thought looking at the funereal face of Allan St. Clair of R.R. 2, Spanish River, Ontario. His face told her nothing but the clerk thought, for sure he had never had to grind away at any substance as she had. He had not had to look at his face daily seeing the things people had attached to it. But then again she thought how would she know. Gut feeling, she said aloud. Gut feeling, she said, to the bales and the aphids and the midges and all the insects who had gathered on her papers.

The girls in her relay team had spun her around with
them and they had all ring-a-ring-a-rosied around the track
as if the girls who came first did not in fact win, only the
girls who came second were important. And it was always
the girls who came second as the clerk thought now, who
really came first. The girls who had fallen, and recovered
and who had aches in their shins and braces on their teeth
and raggedy garments. But the clerk could not remember
if she thought it then or delighted in it then. She hoped
that she had because today she knew for sure. There they
were in their second-place world whirling around the track,
until their House-mistress asked them for a little decorum.
Then they giggled and giggled the whole afternoon
walking home and saying how the clerk saved them from
looking bad, and how fast the clerk was and how she blew
by two Houses like she was on fire. The clerk lived in that
fire all the way to the end of primary school and the fire
seemed to have burned off that malicious interjection she
had heard running down the track. And anyway the clerk
wasn't sophisticated enough then to understand it. She
put it down to the wind on that day. Or then again it may
have been the blood rushing through her veins and
pounding in her ears. She remembered her face felt so hot
it was cold. And ever since then the clerk loved to run.
She put it down to these things, a push to do better at
everything despite everything. You can see her traipsing,
skipping among the bales of paper, dashing up one side
and diagonally across another.

And these days she reads the obituaries because in the obituaries there was a lengthy life crushed into a few sentences as the author and the author's family would crush hers into parentheses.

Docile bodies

Why. What made the dictatorship in Argentina steal people's children? What a strange and ghoulish intimacy they had with the young people they tortured and murdered.

I saw a wall of photographs too at the Museum of Memory and Human Rights, Avenida Matucana in Santiago. I said, oh my god. I sat for some time.

VERSO

Ants send their aged to war.

My legs, and at the end of my legs were black patent
leather shoes. Why is it you only see fragility? Like the
wrists of a girl hanging in a mother's hand, or a boy's
eyelashes falling on his cheek? Everywhere you see
fragility.

What makes the police kill Black children, everywhere?
Rifle through their clothing, write down their names, slap
their faces, rough up their bodies, eat away their young
days, breath in their breaths; wipe their hands on their little
chests and along their legs, and clasp their wrists so tightly
they atrophy. What a strange and ghoulish intimacy.

Last evening a man jumped out of the dark and asked me if
I had any change to spare. I had some coins but I said no.
Out of fear. I wanted to give them to him but I said "no, I
don't have any today." He had startled me and I was afraid
of his homelessness, jumping out in the late evening like
that. I walked on quickly and he called after me, "god bless
you miss, god bless you." I wanted to turn around and give
the coins to him after all but I didn't, I said thank you.
He'd given me a blessing and I'd given him nothing. A
block later I finally remembered his face. I had been
self-indulgent with fear. A block later I remembered his
face. He had seemed exhausted.

The baby next door was in full voice last night. I didn't want to put him in that last verso. It would have injured him. Before I fell asleep he woke up and gave a full-throated account of the hours of dreaming he had, he didn't hush for anything, and not until he was finished. I love his voice, it gives every raw emotion. He must be still alarmed at the stark dry air he entered when he was born. To be born, to be shoved out of water, though that water was diminishing and the body wanting some substance it did not yet know. He awakened again at 3 a.m. with the same desire, or was it rage at not being able to stand and go get what he wanted himself. And then at 6 a.m. He never sounds sad. It is not pity that he is searching for. He sounds energetic and full of life while everyone is in that dark nine-month sleep he escaped. He is full of blood and living. He holds nothing back; his voice is all he has. It has not learned to round itself or square itself on a letter of the alphabet, he is before alphabets. In fact, it is plain to the baby that Marshall McLuhan knew what he was talking about when he said the alphabet was the first technology. But why bring up McLuhan, the baby predates McLuhan. At the same time, right this minute, the baby postdates McLuhan. McLuhan never existed and will not exist in this baby's present. To throw a linguist in, if we think about it, the baby is on one side of Chomsky's universal grammar theory and the people who take care of him are on the other. They are not yet his parents in these new weeks, they are not yet a noun, they do not yet predicate. For the briefest sliver of a second if we understand time this way, they are a hypothesis. His voice rips out with all its intelligence. He seems aware that some others exist and they are there to make that part of him, which he has no control over yet, to make that part of him sensible to him. These others, they quiet him for their own peace. I love the baby's voice. I will have to put my ear to the wall to hear him. He has such originality.

FOUR

You are essence and then you become imperfect, the clerk
says. Why is this? the author asks. Dunno, the clerk replies,
I'm only the clerk and this is all I know. I have been taught
how to be perfect, but not how to live. The author as usual
feels implicated in this. I don't mind, the clerk quickly
decides. This tendency for self-implication in the author
only elicits more leaves and at this moment the clerk is
inundated, thinking of the smell of the earth the author has
just brought in with her. The ground smelled like fresh
ploughed earth outside the Robarts Library and the clerk
thought of the books inside and how, collected there in
stacks, they have returned to their original selves as trees
and earth, and how difficult it must be for them to be
wrenched open again and again to be read and read even
as they are returning, reaching through each other and the
concrete boat around them. That is why it smells like new
ploughed ground around the library. The author brings this
smell with her sometimes, it is on her fingers and in her
hair as if she's done some work in dirt and then reached for
her head absentmindedly.

Once, I sat at a bedside in a hospital, it was a big hospital in San Fernando. It was a small hospital, at least it became small after forty-six years of perspective but then it was a big hospital. There was the scent of Dettol when one approached it and the scent of unhealed sores, and there were efficient nurses in blue stiff cotton dresses and white nurses' caps. They also wore black shoes. This hospital was near to a wharf and overlooked a bay in a Gulf. At the time, to me it was simply the sea. The sea lay at the back of the hospital, and the beach there was not good for swimming. It was said they threw bandages from sores and waste from sickness into the ocean. Of course that could not have been true. This hospital was quiet, *silence* was written near the doorway. There was a room in the hospital on the third or fifth floor. And there lay my grandmother dying. When I entered the room, I could see underneath the beds. It was a general ward, my grandmother had a bed near the window on that side that opened onto the sea. If you looked down the three or five floors you could see a parking lot. That day there was a boy in the parking lot and he was wheeling a bicycle around and around. The sea was tranquil. It must have been a Sunday or a Saturday afternoon. The days, the sea seemed always tranquil then. It was quiet. I recall a breeze blowing the bed sheet of my grandmother's bed. And the boy wheeling his bicycle below, and the tranquil sea. It was aquamarine, the sea. There is a way that a sea sometimes has of laying still and quiet. I sat by the window by the bed and asked my grandmother when she would come home. The legs of the bed were iron. The floor had been cleaned thoroughly with a disinfectant and the movement of the bed sheet where it reached for the floor raised the scent to my nostrils. My grandmother's arm I can see now. I can always see. She asked what I saw outside. I said there was a boy below on a bike. She said when she was well she would buy me a bike. I said I could see the sea. She said if I behaved well I would grow up and go away across that sea to America or Canada or somewhere. She made me promise to behave. I promised without conviction. The Gulf was the Gulf of Paria. A long time ago, before that day when I sat beside my grandmother's bed looking out to the aquamarine sea, this gulf was called Golfo de la Ballena. I found this out long after that day. That day it was simply the sea which was tranquil like a Sunday. Seas and days go on in tranquility whatever you are doing, whatever is going on, they have their own sovereignty. The window was to my right, there was a silence after this conversation and we both looked off. There's nothing more to add in this verso. Except the present tense. There were no whales in the Gulf that day. They threw bandages from sores and waste from sickness into the sea. I was in my brown school uniform, I think. It wasn't brown, it was blue and white. A blue skirt, a white blouse. I would have to have been younger to have worn the brown. You are always younger in this type of moment. I have always sat beside this bed in my school uniform looking out to the serene sea.

VERSO 30

Lightning is flashing and the hair of the wisteria is flying in the wind, and the smoke bush is also waving and the *Rudbeckia* and the cherry tree and there is the sound of rain on the roof and there is thunder in a blue sky, some clouds fire pink with the past sun.

That was last evening. This morning before getting out of bed I ingested several venomous editorial letters. They filled my mouth and sutured my esophagus. One of them went like this . . . on second thought, I don't need to record them here, you will have read them.

At the door of the philosopher I stood. Peered in and said to no one there, why am I here? The crisis in the heart of the enlightenment, I heard. Then I heard, the crisis at the heart of modernity.

VERSO 30.2

And I still can't forgive T.S. Eliot for those "dead negroes" in
the river. To come upon a thing like that. The first in a list
of objects followed by the cows, the chicken coops. And
the collective noun, cargo, just before. To come upon a
thing like that so early. Why should I?

Here again we have to turn to Charles Mingus's
Pithecanthropus Erectus. As I read it there is no way of
translating this text yet. Its language rejects a conventional
translation, that is, once you attempt to translate it into the
sense of a language with vowels and consonants say, that
is the sort of language that directs sound in a particular
direction as opposed to another—let us say into the
direction of known conventional languages that we use to
"communicate" with, then you are lost. Or the meaning is
lost to you. But why talk of translation. That is not really
the point. Unless you feel inadequate to your earlier
comparison of Mingus and Plato. Yes, only in conveying
the breadth of the work. Translation was the metaphor not
the thing. I mean. But is it not music, shouldn't you say
someone in that vein? No, *Pithecanthropus* is not music,
let us say, it is sound; it is a text of philosophical charge.
Mingus suggests another territory.

VERSO 32

Here again we have to turn to Charles Mingus's
Pithecanthropus Erectus. As I read it there is no way of
translating this text yet. Its language rejects a conventional
translation, that is, once you attempt to translate it into the
sense of a language with vowels and consonants say, that is
the sort of language that directs sound in a particular
direction as opposed to another—let us say into the
direction of known conventional languages that we use to
"communicate" with, then you are lost. Or the meaning is
lost to you. But why talk of translation. That is not really
the point. Unless you feel inadequate to your earlier
comparison of Mingus and Plato. Yes, only in conveying
the breadth of the work. Translation was the metaphor not
the thing. I mean. But is it not music, shouldn't you say
someone in that vein? No, *Pithecanthropus* is not music, it
is a text of philosophical charge. No periphrasis exists. Its
ineffability demands another larynx.

Plato was a slaveholder. I cannot get past this. I am a barbarian. That is the way it is. People say that is the way it was. Yes, that is exactly the way it was.

My ancestral line to John Locke. When he wrote "An Essay
Concerning Human Understanding," in 1689 he had
already been the Secretary of the Board of Trade and
Plantations. No one disputes this. He had, too, investments
in the Royal African Company, whose holdings along the
Gambia included forts, factories, and military command of
West Africa, etc., . . . etc., . . . No dispute here either. These
statements—an essay on human understanding, and the
board of trade and plantations—these identifiers can lie
beside each other with no discomfort, apparently. But as I
said, I am a soft-hearted person. I cannot get past this. All
and any interpretative strategies are of no help to me. I am
just a lover with a lover's weaknesses, with her manifest of
heartaches.

VERSO 33

There are two embraces, the clerk knows. Poverty has its nostalgias. I am thinking of this when the author appears. She wants to get on with things, get on with what she calls the work.

If I see a patch of corn in front of a house as I did this
morning, or a zinnia bed, or a wrecked mattress leaning on
the side of a house, an emotion overtakes. Not one of sadness
as you may imagine, you being you, but a familiarity, a grace
of some weight. I might even say longing because it occurs
to me that in the zinnia, the desultory mattress, there used
to be hope, not a big hope, but a small one for the zinnias'
success, or the mattress' resurrection—the nights slept on it
and the afternoons spent jumping on it. And then the
scraggle of corn fighting waterless earth. A tendril, present
happiness and an eternal hope, even also, joy.

My sister used to plant corn in the backyard each year
in its season. I remember the first showing of the corn
shoots; the green of them was young and beautiful. If it
is possible to see energy incarnate it was in these shoots.
The earth so black and yielding we felt bountiful; we said
my sister had a good hand. My sister was very protective
of these corn shoots, even more when they became
stalks and then the corn tassel shows and then their
own silk, and then corn itself.

If I see a patch of flowers near a road, surviving heat and
exhaust fumes and boots, a homesickness washes me and I
am standing in the front yard looking at zinnias. They had
to be planted just as the rainy season ended so that when
the dry, hot season came they would flower. Then half of
the front yard was orange and full of butterflies that could
easily be caught and flown with a bit of thread around their

waists. The circumstances in the house behind, the material circumstances, inlay this homesickness. I am homesick for zinnias; I am homesick for scarcity. These two same things.

If I think of the word *fibre*, I am immediately lying at the edge of a mattress on a bed shared by four or five children and I am fighting for the outside and not the middle; equally I am standing on the edge of a room, the floor strewn with coconut coir that has to be teased apart before it is put in a newly stitched sacking. This sacking, made from a coarse cloth called ticking, is sewn on the Hitachi sewing machine in the room and it is sewn into the shape of a mattress. After, it is stuffed with the teased coir, which is called *fibre*. It takes days to tease this fibre since it has been slept on for many months, until October, and has matted together and made itself hard. Everyone in the house does this work of teasing lightness into the fibre again. When the mattress is stuffed with the fibre, you need a large needle that can thread a thin twine and with this needle and thread the mattress is tufted. Then you have a brand new mattress with striped ticking. That is what happens when I hear the word *fibre*.

If I see a patch of corn in front of a house, as I did this morning, or a small zinnia bed or a wrecked mattress forlorn on the side of a house, all this overtakes me.

What the author has. A condition and a state. Situations.
The word *way*, with a number of meanings. A route, or a
course. Distance. An aspect. One point in time and a
procedure. Three masks and one photograph. A kerosene
lamp. A blue bowl full of feathers. A photocopy of two
faces in a frame on the south wall. A misplaced photograph
she finds at times in a mirror. A blue door. Six pairs of
spectacles.

What the author has. No time. No time, no time at all. By
which I mean no time. No time at all.

What the author knows. I will have added for clarification
or withdrawn some detail. I will have parsed the structure
of the sentence and the meaning of the sentence and
reformulated it to resolve some understanding that was
tentative in the first place, but that merely for the sake of
agreeing to a rule of syntax I present as certain. Moreover,
I will have cleaned out all of my doubt, or all of my
prevarication, or all of my timidity. Indefinite and
unbound weight, the clerk murmurs.

What part of this are you letting go, the clerk asks, because
it seems to me none of this belongs on the dock with me.
The clerk is being clerical, she doesn't want to handle every
passing stray thought of the author, let alone every feeling.
Every feeling need not be considered, else there would be
no room left in the world. No room. The author finds it
hard to rise in the mornings, whatever she is carrying lies as
a boulder on her forehead when she opens her eyes,
though it is invisible to anyone else. The clerk thinks it is
mere self-indulgence. The author agrees. But what do you
do with a feeling like that? It is certainly an embarrassment,
to look at a recumbent discarded mattress and feel home-
sick, or as if one had lost some great love.

VERSO 33.3

A ladybird landed on my hand today while I was cutting
the wisteria. Why do you say ladybird, the clerk nags, it is
ladybug. We called them ladybirds when I was a child, the
author says. I've changed enough I will not change that. So
a ladybird landed on my hand today, when I was cutting
the wisteria. Coccinellidae, the clerk mutters, if you really
want to know. The author in her reverie doesn't hear this
Latin correction. She says, it was a sign of good luck when I
was a child, if a ladybird landed on you.

VERSO 34
Amphibrach

I believe in very little anymore. How convenient. When
there was something to believe in you believed and now
there is nothing you believe in nothing. That seems easy to
me. It is easy to believe in something when there is
something to believe in. You said one night there was
nothing left to love. You were in a bar with another poet
and you said this. It is always hard to love when there is
nothing to love, of course. What is the point of loving
when there is everything to love? Isn't the whole idea to
find something where there is nothing? I see the world
bare. I sometimes experience an existential awful soberness.
I used to think that poetry had the force of action and still,
sometimes, in sentimental moments you may find me
waxing on that subject. But it does not have the force of
action, as can easily be proven. Poetry is not even
information. I can no longer vouch for these ambitions.
I know I've said over the years that poetry in its most
profound meaning tries to perform the job of saying that
which needs to be said or thought, to apprehend the
slippery quality of being human. Now, that all sounds
childish and sloppy to me. Now, as opposed to when?

The poem is concerned formally with the qualities of time, materiality, and meaning and has no obligation to the linear or the representative as is often the burden of prose narrative. There's no pre-eminent or presumptive compulsion to construct or transport your reader, only, simply to address them. Story cannot account for existence. Other questions arise from a poem: when-ness, how-ness, what-ness. The clerk recites this from the author's memoirs. When was I that naive? asks the author.

To calibrate sound, sense, discipline, passion, line, syntax, meaning, metaphor, rhythm, tone, diction, pressure, speed, tension, weight. Everything, everything, everything, the whole thing, in one line, in one moment, the clerk's recitation continues. I depend on something so thin, says the author, so thin.

I do not witness the violence of war, I witness the violence of spectacle. This is what she tells the clerk. Neruda and Lorca, she says, witnessed in their work the violence of war. They told us what we did not know and suggested that if we did know we would respond as better human beings. We do know and we are not better human beings because we no longer respond to knowing as better human beings might. No longer, asks the clerk. In the author's papers, the clerk visits the actual sites of war as the televisual, the Internet, the newspapers. The author is the site of war. This is a metaphor, the clerk asks. No, it is not a metaphor. How can I tell you.

VERSO 35

The sea is oscillant, the waves heave like the back of the
number 3; the clerk climbs out, looks back at the dock, the
freight, the whole enterprise, the temblous archive. When
I was, . . . the author begins. I hate the past, the clerk
concludes that sentence. But we would not . . . Precisely
my point, the clerk says, disappearing over the undulant
back of the number 3, again.

VERSO 35.1

Blue acts, blue ethic, violet surplus, the clerk says, the
clerk says with her pen between her teeth, better violet,
violet sleep.

VERSO 35.2

The clerk mumbles more and more these days and more
and more the author visits the clerk and listens to the clerk
murmuring analgesic violet, early blue. What is all that
noise, she asks. Violet respite, gravitational violet, the clerk
continues. When you are finished, the author shouts, we
must continue. Blue respiration, stapled violet.

Pictures that the blue clerk has. One of the author, against a pyramid, with black short hair. One, against the North Sea. One against the Atlantic at 49 degrees north, and one at 7 degrees north, and one at 10 degrees south, then at the Indian Ocean and the Niger Delta and the Mekong. Then, after a broken-down bus on the way to Kumasi, in a field with other people, one of them looking away from the author.

One hundred and seventy thousand odd nouns after the
colour blue or violet, such as blue maximums, blue wine,
blue safety, blue havoc, blue speed, blue marrow, blue
steering, blue disciplines, blue opportunities, blue reload,
blue diastole. Violet metre, violet scissors. Violet dialysis,
violet suspension, violet incarceration, violet haunch, violet
cancellation, violet systole, violet visas, violet emergencies,
blue snares, etc. . . .

(Things the blue clerk has.) Two bottles of ink, one stapler, one statue of Ganesha, six thousand seven hundred and thirty-one pens, five blotters, a slate board and slate pencil around her neck. Also the way to conjugate verbs in at least three languages; and the sound of ringing; a view of a fountain in a garden behind a doorway.

She lost the veined blue book of her thoughts. The one
book she wrote herself. In the desert between San Pedro de
Atacama and Calama and falling asleep she thought, how
will I reconstruct it all. No, that is for the author. The
notebook, she thought, was full of blueness anyway. Blue
limits. The desert will dry it. Don't worry. The desert will
choose which mirage the blue book will enter—a harbour,
a volcano, the salt corals, the sulphuric algae. The blue clerk
felt peace with this accounting. The clay and the dust went
by, the sand mounded and drifted slowly in their million
years. The experiments of the blue clerk in the lithium
mines and the three villages with the drill and the four hats
and the left plane engine, all this arrived with the clerk at
Valparaíso with its lit morning harbour. There were grey
naval ships there and a pilot vessel coming in continuously
for the bales of grey paper, the flare of red leaves.

Is it the same dock? Valparaíso is so beautiful she wants
to remain there, ride the funiculars up and down their
particular streets, walk into a shoe shop. There are the gulls,
the faint ship on the horizon. The clouds from the window
are cobalt cranes.

VERSO 37.1

When I lost the blue book of your blue thoughts I was, at
first, afraid. These were documents I felt I had lost and
would never find again. Evidence of my collections, my
thoughts, yes. But then my vertebrae, my vertebrae or it
seemed as if my bones, my ribs left their place and walked
into someone else. Someone calmer. Anyway I knew that I
could summon it all again, and anyway what was in the
book was all my past anxieties, and I had lost them before
the bus rode out of the desert toward the airport after I saw
the smallest Malva field.

VERSO 38

I looked into the same mirror as Neruda, I touched his
telephone, his hairbrushes; peered at his briefcases. *Te
recuerdo como eras en el último otoño. . . . y las hojas caían
en el agua de tu alma* . . . this far this distance, sun's going,
Avenida Constitución. I saw a walking baby in Bella Vista.
These are the notes the clerk deciphers.

VERSO 38.1

These are Ho Chi Minh's spectacles. I took a photograph.
I took a photograph of his sandals. I walked in a quiet line
into his vault containing his translucent body. A child and
her mother pointed to my face and laughed. I did the same
to them.

VERSO 38.2

On the subway from Pedro de Valdivia to La Moneda as
from Yonge to Warden, still, the sleeping commuter
between home and work, the universal handbag. In the
deep, deep sleep of tyrannies, the long, long sleep of
oppressions. Look at our faces, we are ready to abandon
everyone else for the violent domestic eases.

On the road after Calama. On a road like this you don't
know where you are. Whether you have arrived or whether
you are still on your way. Whether you are still at the
beginning or at the end. You are in the middle all the time.
What would be the sign?

There was a piece of paper flying by in the desert. From
where to where. From the air the desert is a brown paper
with lines and wrinkles. On the ground you are at the
beginning forever or in the middle or at the end. The clerk
may choose right this minute to step out of the car and
walk into another room, another atmosphere. Along the
way men are scraping up the desert floor looking for
something. Some lost object. I can see their nails from here,
the sunglasses, the leather boots and belt buckles. Will they
find the button they lost, a nugget of their hearts, or the
stone of water buried there?

Echinopsis atacamensis lurch out of the Andes, prickled,
long-necked. And the road is made of salt to Caixa.

I travel the subway, the first time in years. There, on the
train, I meet my early self, my young and tender self. A
young woman in her twenties in a dress with thin straps
under a thin coat. She has a book and a straw bag and a
face so dedicated to itself, so certain, that it falls asleep on
the train so safely as if the train is not harmful, will not be
harmful, will stop where the woman wants it to stop, as if
the woman will awake when she arrives at her destination,
even if she is in a deep sleep and the stop is two stations
away, even if it is five stations away. Her face is innocent of
any failures. Or it is a face committed to failures as if
failures will be the joy. No, it is a face empty of the meaning
of failure. Why failure, what will be failed. My tenderest
self, the author says, my tenderest self was the self that felt
everything newly, all experience freshly. Today everything
has the sediment of experience, the cumulus of event
tinges the new experience, or summarizes it before it is felt,
or alters it before it is observed. But then, I was in my
tender self on the subway on a Saturday morning or any
time of day, because time was unimportant or time was
merely the space where new things could happen.

   After those tender and volatile days all is summary,
even love. My tender self sat on the train, fell asleep
between stops. She was going to a friend's apartment, she
had an earring in one ear, her hair was loose, her wrist
delicate with bangles, all the certainty and uncertainty of
tenderness, kindness, brightness, newness glowed on her

sleeping face. She was ready for the world, nothing was behind her, everything was ahead; even in the months and years to come, even when she passed them everything was still ahead of her; the self looking at her, the one who is the author is behind her. She is an unassailable ache in the author, a lover, not a yearning but a love.

The author loves this tender self because this tender self is unassailable, undiminished, unsedimented, raw and conscious. Sinuous. Without second thoughts, without doubt. At a certain stop the author exits the train. She could stay on but she does not want this tender self to open her eyes and see the author observing. She wants that woman to go on to her life unattended by misgivings. Even a look from the author would blight the woman. That is how potent the author's looks have become. The tender woman seated there, sleeping her beautiful sleep, has an instinctive clarity that the author will, over time, make too laser-like, too atomic. If the author stays and if the tender woman wakes and sees the author staring, the tender woman will not be able to avoid the acidic routes she'll have to cross. So the author leaves her tender self on the train.

VERSO 40

If you are in a hotel on the sixth floor and you move to
the window, you are not in the salt lake with the dancing
flamingos. In the salt lake with the dancing flamingos,
the quiet is quiet, the desert is quiet, the absence is quiet,
the quiet is quiet. Quiet of some beings like yourself.
Quiet of some beings like myself, and you wish to join
that quiet not as yourself but as yourself before yourself.
I needed quiet.

I loved the desert. Unusable word—loved, but I loved the
desert, the quiet. I felt a peace in it, not harmless or fragile.
I felt even. Level. I only fear other human beings, not the
world. Not the earth. There I am willing to be devoured by
its silence, its bird, its animal, its salt. Willing, resigned. But
human beings, of a kind, the ones headlong, ripping the
organism of the planet apart, they chill me. Anyway the
desert is beautiful, there are mirages of harbours and seas
in it, or was it the oceans, the crust, the magma, the
stratosphere's reflection, or a looking glass, un espejo.

VERSO 40.1.1

There. What romanticism. I could leave the desert. I could but I didn't want to leave. I wished you didn't want to leave. Yes, I wished that. But there was a moment when I wanted to stay there, knowing I could leave. It was the closest I had come to staying anywhere.

VERSO 40.1.2

I walked from Machuca toward San Pedro de Atacama
beside a strict river. I could have walked on and on and
on. At the same time twenty-seven children were
slaughtered in Connecticut. If we are not witnessing an
insane society we are insane. I am insane walking this
Atacama road from Machuca. An infection.

VERSO 40.2

I have a photo of me who is me, and then there is the me who is me.

Conquest makes the life of the conquered seem brief. This I
thought in Museo Larco after being overwhelmed by the
breadth of the Inca Empire. And those the Inca conquered
must have felt the shortening of their existences too. When
the Spanish arrived the thousands of years of the Inca
collapsed into one earthen bowl. All their lives collapsed
into one life. A summary.

VERSO 40.4

This morning from my hotel window I saw a carrion
bird eating something on a rooftop. A pigeon was there
a moment before but when I lifted my head from some
distraction it was the coal-coloured carrion bird I
remembered from my childhood—from neck to crown it
was bald. I learned in my childhood its featherless head
and cowl served the purpose of dipping into a carcass
without becoming soiled or at least viscera would not stick
to its scavenging head. To evolve this way. I could not see
the body it was eating. When it was done it left. It was a
lone bird.

VERSO 40.5

Summary. There is a photo of Monk and Nellie and
Coltrane. It is not possible for me to describe the five
centuries it took to record this image.

M sent me a photograph by Daguerre. It is of the first
human being to be photographed. Someone is cleaning the
shoes of someone. All descriptions of the photograph claim
that the first human being to be photographed is the figure
having his shoes cleaned. I see first the figure cleaning the
shoes as the photograph's subject. Secondly, the event of
the shoe-cleaning. From this immediately I saw the state of
the world.

Tonight my brain is full of beautiful things collected over three weeks: the ring around Jupiter in the southern hemisphere; three flamingos dancing brine shrimp to the surface; the mirages of harbours only I have seen; the lithium salt desert; the rush for the local train at Ollantaytambo; a frantic scramble for a bundle of goods left behind; the electrochemical sky. The silence was the best thing.

VERSO 41.1

This is what I am saying, the blue clerk says, violet begins.
There is this about my job, the day is a bright one, the sea
billowing. Today we are on the Pacific. We arrived last
night by the grey and violet sea. The bales drove us like old
sails. The aphids dove in the shape of anchors. I smelled
twelve thousand desert flowers. We were joined by one
million bees, they slept in the folds of our documents,
the oil barges watered in our eyes, the wires braceleted the
great music of the ocean.

I am not really in life, the author says. I am really a voyeur.
But the part of me that is in life is in pain all the time.
That's me, says the clerk. You watch, I feel. I'm sure that
some philosopher has examined this, assures the clerk.
I am sure that there are theories about it, the author replies,
but I don't care. I know all about it and knowing that a
philosopher has written about it gives me no peace.
Knowing that it has been gone over in many languages
gives you no rest. In fact, it gives me even more pain,
because it means there is no remedy. I need a pill for this,
I need an antioxidant. Even philosophers have it. Pain, I
mean. Once, in my twenties, I knocked on the door of a
philosopher. He was a scholar of Habermas. I knocked on
the door and he did not answer at first, so I knocked again.
He opened the door as if he had been asleep; the room was
dark with his papers and his research. They gave off a dust,
a gloom where I thought they may have given off a light,
an illumination. He appeared disturbed, then looking at me
he said, sorry, but he had been meditating. I was shocked.
I was in my twenties, I could still be shocked. I had tried
meditation to no avail. I had thought philosophy would
give me peace. I was shocked but I also felt a little superior.
Or at least suddenly we were on the same level despite
his far superior grasp of such theories as instrumental
rationalization. So I thought if he is meditating what is
left for me.

VERSO 42.1

I went to the door of the philosophers too, the clerk
stutters.

The crisis at the heart of modernity is, you asked. I
cannot find my presentation, do not introduce Kant and
Blumenbach here. Their romance. What fictions. Their
skulls. Violet terminals have appeared in the violet hours
I have spent, the violet bookkeeping has been done,
violet officials have declared the violet kilometres' violet
shoulders.

The clerk covers the faces of every clock in the room in Miraflores. The author uncovers them. The clerk covers them again. I cannot sleep with all the clocks lit up like daylight, she says. And why are there so many? I've lived with the energy of clocks, the author says, they invigorate a room even in sleep. I've lived with them in all my rooms, among piles of paper, the new construction of shelves, between bricks and plastic crates and wood and imaginary numbers. The clerk is sleepless with clocks, she hates the red glow or the blue glow or the green glow of clocks, especially at night when they beam out their increments of time and time and time and time; they shatter the eyelids. I had no dear house where I always went, she said, only screaming apartments and rooms, moulting. I was thrown into the world nuclear and nautical. People have no idea the effects they have on other people—everything shatters, everything breaks to the touch. Wisteria this summer, the green job of the wisteria I watched all summer. The early feathers of the smoke bush, and the open mathematics of the weeds, nameless, and the insecticideless lilacs and the multiplying sparrows.

VERSO 44

In the author's world, every aspect of life is an emergency.
The body is an emergency. I think you've said this many
times. The clerk disappears into the belly of paper on the
wharf, searching. The clerk has filed all the paper in block
stowage. Sometimes the author comes here and things
become misplaced. It is usually when the clerk is dozing,
that is not often. The air on the wharf is as full of oxygen
as a casino. The clerk knows where the emergency is,
where the anger is, where the salt, where the sugar,
where the flowers.

I am washed in this emergency, the author says. I wake
up in emergency. Perhaps if you can be more explicit, says
the clerk, returning overladen and invisible behind a
four-foot stack of leaves. These leaves are heavier than they
look. A word is not an easy thing, it is not a light thing.
Others would think the clerk is magical, the tonnage doesn't
seem to bother her. You would sink under its weight.

If I have said this many times, it makes it no less true,
no more understandable, the author continues. If I were
to take this body outside this minute, outside of where you
and I live you would see the alarms it sets off. Then I am
flooded with adrenaline, this adrenaline is killing me; my
system cannot take it to be always flooded in adrenaline.
At times it runs down my left side all day, then every skin
cell vibrates with pain. You understand, this pain is physical
but I know it emanates from the sirens that are turned on,
that come alive whenever we step outside, you and I.

You and I, the clerk says, after pausing for a moment, after feeling the full weight of the tonnage. But this is not something the clerk can feel, the clerk tells herself; to feel this weight would be to misinterpret the archive or to dispute her responsibilities in the archive. Here then, she says, going back to her job, here I have it. 1955, you first recorded this emergency. '55? the author questions, I wasn't writing then. The author peers knowingly at the clerk. Has the clerk been infected with this emergency too but in hindsight? I wasn't writing then, she puts her hand tenderly on the clerk's inky shoulder. But I was collecting, says the clerk and reads out the gradatios of the decades of emergency.

I have here the sense of orange, and the sense of distances, then a sound of a window falling shut. There is great blinding sunlight and a wall of air to your left, then the smell of flour in oils. The records begin with these. There is a river and a lost shoe. There is always, of course, an ocean, the songs of volumes of water and scuttling sand. And here the escarpment of a yellow house dividing the world, when you understood the word but, and here your face caved in when you ingested the thought. Stop, says the author.

Who is this fucking Horace? Someone you once studied.
Was forced to study you mean! Whatever, forced, made to,
obliged, irrelevant. It's all part of you now like so many gut
microbes. You may be sanguine about it . . . For once the
clerk laughs into a blood-blue hand, Sanguine, you might
say that, like blood. Anyway you have a note from Horace
somewhere. The clerk is only playing, she knows exactly
where. She flits wraithlike, wrath-like, brushing gnats away,
a new infestation of snakes slough off their skins to make
twine when she approaches. She traipses to the very back
of the madrepore. The author hears her humming—a
variation of irox, red oxide, sombre, rubia tinctorium. The
clerk, despite the weight of things, loves her work or, one
might say, because the clerk is a creation of the work she is
indefinable from the work or, one might say, the work is
indefinable from the clerk or, better still, the work is the
clerk. And so the clerk, in this sense, when she is chal-
lenged or called upon to produce some misstep of the
author, is happy. Here deep in the bales of paper she blows
a sand of indecipherable-ness from a crumbling pile and
skips back the long wharf to where the author stands. *Rage,*
she quotes, *Rage armed Archilochus with the iambic of his
own invention.* You used to love that line.

We are in the age of nerves, the author quotes in reply. Yes,
yes, Huidobro then. Here he is, here he is, the clerk soothes,
Estamos en el ciclo de los nervios. This is closer to the
language. The author breathes, *Invent new worlds and
watch your word*. The clerk translates, *Inventa mundos
nuevos y cuida tu palabra*. So the clerk goes on with her
humming. Violet toll roads, freezing violet, museums of
blue, violet turbines, blue visas.

Why do you talk like that? Where did you get that voice? It
is evening on the wharf. Crepuscular, as in Thelonius
Monk's "Crepuscule With Nellie." I collected it, said the
author. Gathered it. From everything, from the walks to
and from schools, past funeral homes, past dumpsters,
past canefields, past ladies selling flour; from gazing, from
listening, kicking surf, being tumbled in sand, being cut
with nails and broken shells, from running barefoot on hot
asphalt, from quarrels, in noisy bars, in suicidal quiet, past
gloom, with sugar, past trees with rangy leaves, pierced ears,
with sour cherries in the throat, wasps, ants, scraping ice on
a windscreen, past water, cutlasses, sewers, after Wednesday,
after spoons. When sleeping I collected the end of breath-
ing. Then salt, then oranges, light switches, farine; from
cemeteries, from little streets, past long grass, razor grass,
fever grass, brilliant muscles oiled in sweat, from water, from
work, from hearing, donkeys, bananaquits mostly, from the
loneliest most poisonous smell of *Cestrum nocturnum*;
from the sound of shaved ice with red syrup, bottles, broken
bottles, green broken bottles, chairs, peppers. Stop. Why?
You and your endless lists, why? I don't fully know why.
Must I? Why don't we take it on the face of it? Lists exist
and they may be consecutive or serial or alternative on the
other hand they may be important as exquisite objects on
their own or as an alternate spelling of everything. As you
say. I thought you would like the idea of lists. To continue
then, why do you speak that way? Because of water, the

reef out there, the *Fregata magnificens*, look at the boiling turquoise, the sea's albumen. Because the throat fills with thick reeds, drowned fine pebbles, because of stairs' gradient, the way corn is disappearing, steep terraces. Grapheme teeth, on the cold walls and the stringy aortas, a thousand musics.

It is morning on the wharf, the author has gone on this way well into the night and now it is morning. The author and the clerk speaking in their sleep. At times nouns were hunted by prepositions followed by an adjective. They sat up suddenly like the dead, then lay down with the anxiety of the thought that they were alive after all. The dock creaked, the papers bloomed blue letters. Their sleep was the jittery sleep of birds. They had long arms. Long, long arms. If only. Alphabets were used up and used up and lay flat and slumped, and dishevelled of their normal shapes.

It's useless to speak any other way, the author says in a morning voice. Useless, says the clerk. The night passed in more nouns.

Violet. This is what the clerk thinks. Violet hand, violet
notes, violet metre, violet hammer, violet bed, violet
scissors, violet management, violet speed, yes with violet
speed, violet washers, violet sleep, violet percent, taken
violet yesterday, violet incarceration, violet ambulances,
immediate violet, violet labour, intended violet, violet
transcripts, suspended violet for now, violet cancels, blind
violet, violet schemes, reply violet

VERSO 49

There were two kinds of books. Books of discomfort and
books of discomfort. The books of discomfort said the "you"
that you think you are is not the you that you are; and the
books of discomfort said you are the you that you are,
though, you are also the you that you think you are, which
is not the you that you think you are.

When I was small they lived over the hill and over the highway and down some stone stairs. They lived in a house with our grandmother. And they were eight of them and they were my sisters and brothers and cousins. I lived in a room over the hill with my mother and two brothers and my father. The hill was steep and the road had to be crossed before getting to the hill. The road was busy with cars and I was small. The stone steps were steep too but the house made them easy. When I was small I lived on my mother's hips and in my father's long arms. And they lived over the hill with the highway between us and the stone steps. They seemed happy. They were the big ones. I lived with my brothers with my father and mother. We were the little ones. They were the lucky ones. We lived on our mother's hips and in our father's long arms. Our mother and father tore each other apart sometimes. They fought and fought and spilled drinks on the floor until they fell asleep. That is how they loved each other. At the beginning of each week they were calm and at the end of each week they were angry. The beginning of the week we were noisy, the end of the week we were quiet. My sisters and brothers who lived over the hill and over the highway and down the stone steps hugged us when we arrived and cried when we left. We cried too when our mother took us away. Our mother and father lived in a room beside a field.

Those aphids I put in an early verso or two, they appeared
in my real garden. All summer I sprayed them with soap,
they haven't left. Then I made out their writing. *The Wire*
is the latest version of *The Adventures of Huckleberry Finn*.
An old fable, digitized for the age. Vonnegut said there
were only so many plotlines. Whose plotlines are these?
Well, not ours, of course. On our side nobody gets out of
the hole, nobody gets the girl. There are only rags and no
riches. Those aphids I put in an early verso or two, they
appeared in my real garden. All summer I sprayed them
with soap, they haven't left. I made out their writing.

VERSO 51.1

"We are now crossing the Andes," the pilot said. There was a dry riverbed running through the bare majestic buckle of mountains, the dust snow, the dry barren inclines, folded, brown clay silt, the wealth, the rage of mountains, then a green lake. We are crossing the Andes, please fasten your seat belt.

In the Museum there is a gallery of erotica of the Inca
Empire. How long the fascination with the sexual body and
how common. Did the king collect these like today's
pornography in a footlocker or is that the judeo-christian-
islamic thought that warps the body's pleasures. Yet the
king was the king. Can the body be free of power. The body
is never the body, the author says, and we are always
referring to the female body. Why the eternal fascination,
the clerk wonders, perhaps like all power it must be kept,
held, battled for, there is an antagonist, the war is never
over. I do not know what to do with that first sentence,
says the clerk, I did not know what to do with that
sentence, says the author. That is all that I wrote in my
notebook that day, the day when I took the taxi from
Miraflores to the Larco. The gallery of erotica is tucked
away from the main galleries, as if it contains something
incendiary. And so, strangely, when I entered it I giggled.
The bodies were arranged in pairs for the most part,
reclining or standing in some representation of copulation;
most were of a man and a woman, a few of two men which
the museum labeled as a man and a woman. None of two
women. There was one of a woman alone, standing, her
vagina open and large as the surface of her body. All of the
bodies were thick, substantial, asymmetrical, real.

Most days the clerk herself is quiet. What with the constant noise of the author, that is the quiet of the clerk. When she arrived on the bank of the Chao Phraya River, the author found everything as she had imagined. The fortuneteller said, "You are a teacher, you have been married, you are not good with that; it is very bad, you shouldn't be married." She sat by the food-seller and watched the irregular monks go by, the monk she had put in a novel strolled along in his tattoos looking as dangerous as ever. He didn't even look at her; he went on with his life where she had left off and where she could not imagine. The food-seller brought fish and rice and she sat at a low little table eating in a satisfied and happy way, the food seller smiled at her as if welcoming her home. She sat there among the broken-down tiny shops in the lanes at the back of the river and it was as if she was home in one of her pages. The dust of graphene covered her hands like ornaments. Ointment.

The clerk is noiseless, intent on the marsupial sighs of each
letter of the alphabet. A cyst in the floor of the mouth, a
ruptured salivary gland. The marsupialization of the ranula,
cutting a slit into an abscess. Allowing the sublingual gland
to re-establish its connection with the oral cavity. This is
how the author explains when the clerk tells her of the
marsupial sighs, of the alphabet. Ah, she says. Within the
letter a, for example, a perfect pouch for *adipose*, for *aleph*,
for *amen*, for *ah*, for *water*.

VERSO 54.1

The troop of buyers has arrived; the loaded boats slip out to
the Mediterranean. A slow night. Floating.

When I finally arrived at the door of no return, there was
an official there, a guide who was a man in his ordinary life,
or a dissembler. Exhausted violet, the clerk interjects. Yes,
says the author. Violet snares. He arranged himself at the
end of the story. Violet files. Violet chemistry. Violet unction.
It was December, we had brought a bottle of rum; some
ancient ritual we remembered from nowhere and no one.
We stepped one behind the other as usual. The castle was
huge, opulent. We went like pilgrims. You were pilgrims.
We were pilgrims. This is the holiest we ever were. Our
gods were in the holding cells. We awakened our gods, and
we left them there, since we never needed gods again. We
did not have wicked gods so they understood. They lay in
their corners, on their disintegrated floors, they lay on their
walls of skin dust. They stood when we entered, happy to
see us. Our guide said, this was the prison cell for the men,
this was the prison cell for the women. I wanted to strangle
the guide. As if he were the original guide. It took all my
will. Yet in the rooms the guide was irrelevant. The gods
woke up and we felt pity for them, and affection, and love.
They felt happy for us, we were still alive. Yes, we are still
alive, we said. And we had returned to thank them. You are
still alive, they said. Yes, we are still alive. They looked at us
like violet; like violet teas they drank us. We said, here we
are. They said, you are still alive. We said, yes, yes, we are
still alive. How lemon, they said, how blue like fortune. We
took the bottle of rum from our veins, we washed their

faces, we sewed their thin skins. We were pilgrims, they were gods. They said with wonder and admiration, you are still alive, like hydrogen, like oxygen.

We all stood there for some infinite time. We did weep but that is nothing in comparison.

VERSO 56

This is what the clerk thinks: lemon documents, lemon
factors, then lemon, watch lemon, lemon nails, wasp lemon,
lemon summary, slap lemon, lemon dangers, lemon
crevasses, there are a few documents that came, lemon
defections, why allow a certain kind of speech, lemon
vines, lemon ankles, distance lemon, lemon knotting, bay
lemon, lemon reaches. This is what we have.

Violet kilometres, violet snares, violet bookkeeping, violet whimpers, official violet, probationary violet, scabrous violet, violet early, violet itself, violet becomes, violet gravity, violet respiration, better violet, violet terminals, violet asylum, criminal violet, violet coast, this is what the clerk thinks.

I was one of three wives in Cairo, one of three Blacks in
Hanoi, one of ten on a suspension bridge, one of two
people. I left my Pa at the Ossington subway station.
At the tomb of Ho Chi Minh someone touched my hair.
Not everyone wants immortality, or longevity, or to know
the meaning of life. Only freedom matters.

VERSO 58.1

"But, Madame, are we not human, can we not speak?" This, from a silver seller in Khan el-Khalili in Cairo. Are we not human, can we not speak.

VERSO 58.2

"Do you want a little something, a little amusement?"
This, from a stranger at a sweets stall. "You don't want a
little something?"

VERSO 59

A quieting, but a busy kind of quiet. A rich quiet. I love to wake up around 5 a.m., go down to my reading chair, turn the light on and read. But there are rules.

Violet ambulances, violet openings, violet terminals,
violet hours, weather's violet, populist violet. This is what
the clerk says, blue-ribbed. Blue quarrels, blue diastole,
blue steering, blue expenses, blue mileage, blue havoc,
blue appliance, blue creeks. The clerk continues, the sedge
of blue.

VERSO 59.2

Passengers may leave small parcels or packages in charge
of the collectors of stations . . . packages of luggage so left
will only be delivered up to the party presenting the
receipt granted

The reading regimen is as follows—while writing poetry,
read philosophy or natural history; while writing fiction, read
poetry; after, but not before or during writing poetry, read
fiction. These rules of reading keep the compartments of
poetry and prose fiction pristine. It is really the poetry that
demands this regimen, it is a fragile and impressionable art
so all means have to be employed to protect it from excess
while feeding it with infusions of practical, scientific, and
philosophical propositions. Almanacs.

Every listing generates a new listing. Every map another road.

FORM AND/OR REFERENCE TO

POLITICAL PLACES

LANGUAGE

Verso 32.1

Verso 32.2

Verso 34.1 (the concerns of the poem)

Verso 44 (the archive; the word)

Verso 45 (b/c "Rage armed Archilochus . . .")

Verso 53 (the dust of grapheme)

Verso 54

NOTES ON THE HUMAN

(Toward the diacritical as well. The stress not just on a word but
on a being. Making the human. Making the unhuman. The
author's left side, the line on her face, the human zoos.)

Verso 17 (War Series and "Venus")

Verso 40.5 (Monk, Nellie, Coltrane photo—shares same number
with the following)

Verso 40.6 (Daguerre)

NATION | THE DOOR

Verso 5.1 (newly numbered . . . beginning In December)

Verso 5.5

Verso 10.1

Verso 17

Verso 17.2

Verso 22

Verso 27

Verso 32.2 (Locke)

THE SEARCH AND ARCHIVES (JOHN BRAND AND
BENJAMIN/BAUDELAIRE) THE SEARCH AND WHAT IS
NOT/OR IS NOT REVEALED/THE ARCHIVE AND THE
CLERK'S TAKE ON THAT

Verso 16.1 (Benjamin / Baudelaire)

The clerk notes, even Angela Carter's reconstruction fails in the
sentence that continues ". . . she clutched an enormous handful
of dreadlocks to her pubic mound." What madness is that?

Verso 22 (John Brand)

BRAITHWAITE | JABÈS | BENJAMIN | ELLISON | STEIN

Verso 13.1

Verso 16

Verso 16

Verso 16.1 (Benjamin)

Verso 19.2 (Stein and Toklas)

Verso 21 (Jacques Roumain)

Verso 21.1 (Márquez and Marsalis)

Verso 21.4 (Ellison, *Invisible Man*)

Verso 21.5 (Harris, *Palace of the Peacock*)

Verso 30.2 (T.S. Eliot)

Verso 32.1 (Plato)

Verso 32.2 (Locke)

Verso 34.2 (*Inventory* / Neruda, Lorca)

Verso 45 (Horace)

Verso 46 (Huidobro)

ARTISTS | PAINTERS | MUSICIANS

Verso 3.1 Basquiat

Verso 17 Lam

Verso 18 Lawrence

Verso 20

Verso 21—all iterations

Verso 21 (Roumain)

Verso 21.1 (Márquez)

Verso 31 (Mingus)

Verso 32 (Mingus)

THE CITY

Verso 3.0

Verso 3.1

All of verso 3s

NOTES THE AUTHOR HAS

So many cigarettes, the Clerk smokes, even though the Clerk
does not smoke but Deleuze's voice sounds like 700 cigarettes.
Gilles Deleuze in *L'Abécédaire de Gilles Deleuze—interviews
between* Gilles Deleuze *and* Claire Parnet.

Edmond Jabès translated by Rosmarie Waldrop, *The Book of
Questions: Volume 1.* Aisha Sasha John pointed me here. One
night we were talking and the next morning she sent me Jabès.

Why do you have this fetish with bibliography? the clerk asks.
It's the fever of coloniality, the author answers honestly for once.

The Arcades Project. Walter Benjamin translated by Howard Eiland and Kevin McLaughlin, *The Arcades Project*.

To find the preface, the Clerk had to scour and finally Leslie Sanders called Sergio Villani, a Baudelaire Scholar who found it. André Suarès' 1933 preface to Baudelaire's *Les Fleurs du mal*. Then the Clerk had to have it translated by two people, including Martha B. It took me years, the Clerk said. To tell the truth I was looking for something else in Benjamin when I came upon Suarès. What could it mean?

"Here I am singing," she said, *". . . I have arrived at the great mountain range of the heavens, the power of those who have died comes back to me, from infinity they have spoken to me. Here I am singing."*

The Clerk and the Author went to the Venice Biennale, 2015. They heard the voice of Lola Kiepja; they wept uncontrollably. Word for Word. At the Latin American Pavilion—*Indigenous Voices* it was called.

Charles Mingus—album liner notes—*Pithecanthropus Erectus.*

Gertrude Stein, *The Autobiography of Alice B. Toklas* and Gertrude Stein, *Three Lives*. Christina Sharpe led me to this. The index. Say no more here; please leave it up to me. I have only shown you 59 or so of the Versos. But, one last thing. Degas. I'd forgotten Degas in New Orleans. "And then I love silhouettes so much and these silhouettes walk." His family's wealth came from those silhouettes, as you may imagine.

The Clerk and the Author made notes, different ones on each occasion. 1926 *New York Herald Tribune,* Apollinaire quoted in Apollinaire exhibit, Musée de l'Orangerie, Apollinaire's things, the Clerk wrote.

Wilson Harris, *Selected Essays of Wilson Harris: The Unfinished Genesis of the Imagination.* Austin Clarke led you to him though you never finished reading this. Never but always.

Handwritten note, near his glasses at Neruda's house in Isla Negra "Te recuerdo como eras en el último otoño . . . en sus ojos peleaban las llamas del crespusculo y las hojas caían en el agua de tu alma . . ."

The Horace Anthology: The Odes, The Epodes, The Satires The Epistles, The Art of Poetry. I reminded you about Horace.

Jean Rhys, "Till September Petronella". Impossible to leave that story.

Selected Poetry of Vincente Huidobro by Vicente Huidobro, translated/edited by David Guss.

Kamau Brathwaite, *DS(2) dreamstories.* Very important for dreams, the clerk says. See the public record. The whole category of dreams begins somewhere here.

THE ALMANAC
Trinidad Official and Commercial Register and Almanac January 1882.

RECTOS

Thought for the rectos—there could be / perhaps should be several iterations of them. To appear and disappear the capturing perspective . . .

Verso 25.1 (hmm / another sense of the diacritical / the stress . . .)

UNNUMBERED VERSOS

Verso 2.2 Keep

Also the smell of work somewhere in another verso

Unnumbered versos?

One night in a taxi in Lima, the raw umber lovely night. No lights.

You felt a vast exit on your right shoulder. You said to the driver,

Is there an ocean?

He said, Yes, the Pacific.

Then you both were quiet.

WHAT THE CLERK DOES ON MONDAYS

Mondays the Clerk wakes up

60 *small* mistakes to be corrected

200 incidents of Blue

in her ears

traffic under these circumstances

disciplines

hinges

protein

violet respiration

gorse, lizards, never, coast

written lemon, 66

factors, asylum

VERSO 33.1

If I see a patch of corn, in front of a house as I did this morning, or a zinnia bed, or a wrecked mattress leaning on the side of a house, an emotion overtakes. Not one of sadness as you may imagine, you being you, but a familiarity, a grace of some weight. I might even say longing, because it occurs to me that in the zinnia, the desultory mattress, there used to be hope, not a big hope, but a tendril one for the zinnias' success, or the mattress' resurrection—the nights slept on it and the afternoons spent jumping on it. And then the scraggle of corn fighting waterless earth. A small, present happiness and an eternal hope, even also, joy.

If I see a patch of flowers near a road surviving heat and exhaust fumes and boots, a homesickness washes me and I am standing in the front yard looking at zinnias. The dire circumstances in the house behind, the material circumstances, the poverty, are part of this homesickness. Not because, one, the scarcity, and two, the zinnias, set each other off as some might think, but because they were the same.